Sarah Flower, a leading nutritionist and author of many cookery books, is passionate about healthy eating and is a keen advocate of the sugar-free and low-carb way of eating. She has trained with *The Real Meal Revolution*, originally established by Professor Tim Noakes and Jonno Proudfoot, both of whom advise a Banting/LCHF (low-carbohydrate, high-fat) diet and is now herself a Banting coach in the UK. Sarah writes for a number of publications, including the *Daily Mail*, *Top Santé* magazine and *Healthista*. She appears regularly on BBC Radio Devon.

ALSO BY SARAH FLOWER

The Busy Mum's Plan-Ahead Cookbook

The Sugar-Free Family Cookbook

Eat Well, Spend Less

The Healthy Lifestyle Diet Cookbook

The Healthy Halogen Cookbook

The Healthy Slow Cooker Cookbook

Perfect Baking with Your Halogen Oven

Halogen Cooking for Two

The Everyday Halogen Family Cookbook

The Everyday Halogen Oven Cookbook

Slow Cook, Fast Food

Low-Carb Slow Cooker

Eating to Beat Type 2 Diabetes

Slow Cooker Family Classics

The Keto Slow Cooker

SLOW COOKER: FOR LESS

EASY, BUDGET-FRIENDLY RECIPES FOR THE WHOLE FAMILY

Sarah Flower

ROBINSON

ROBINSON

First published in Great Britain in 2021 by Robinson

A CIP catalogue record for this book
is available from the British Library.

ISBN 978-1-47214-610-6

Designed by Thextension

Typeset in Bely and Bely Display, designed by Roxane Gataud

Printed in Slovenia by DZS Grafik

Papers used by Robinson are from well-managed forests
and other responsible sources.

Robinson
An imprint of Little, Brown Book Group
Carmelite House, 50 Victoria Embankment, London EC4Y 0DZ

An Hachette UK Company
www.hachette.co.uk

www.littlebrown.co.uk

The recommendations given in this book are solely intended
as education and should not be taken as medical advice.

Contents

Introduction

This is my sixth slow cooker book, which, if nothing else, does prove how obsessed I am with these wonderful gadgets. It has been a fascinating few months trying new recipes with budgets in mind. No matter what your budget, it is reassuring to know that we can still make delicious, comforting and affordable home-cooked meals with ease.

My very first book, published in 2009, was a money-saving lifestyle book. At the time I had a column with *My Weekly* on money saving, so the book seemed a good fit. This was followed shortly after by my first cookery book, *Eat Well Spend Less*, where I demonstrated how you could have a healthy diet on a budget. Since then, I have gone on to publish a further twenty books. This book is not a nutritional bible. It contains pure, honest home-cooked food for those on a budget; however, it is important to note that those who cook from scratch are generally healthier than those who buy takeaways or eat processed foods regardless of the fat, carbohydrate and protein content. Real food cooked from scratch is the first and the most important step towards good health. I am a very simple family cook and I use everyday ingredients such as fresh vegetables, meat, herbs, spices and store-cupboard finds such as tinned tomatoes, beans and other pulses. If you check out my store-cupboard chapter, you will find a list of the ingredients used in this book, including the herbs and spices used in many of the recipes. At the beginning of each chapter, you will find a short introduction where I discuss top tips on the chapter that follows. It is important to read these because they include information on how to use the slow cooker or give you ingredients tips such as how to find the right cuts of meat.

If you are new to the slow cooker, or you haven't used one for a while, I do urge you to read my chapter 'How to use your slow cooker' (page 1). They are wonderful machines, but there are some rules to follow to ensure the perfect cook. Please note, all the timings and recommendations in this book are based on a new slow cooker – either my Crockpot Multi Cooker or my Ninja Pro. If you have an older cooker or a different model, you might want to check the temperatures, as these can vary from one machine to another. Older slow cookers can have hot spots where, when on high, things can catch. If this describes your machine, opt for the low setting rather than high, and this can avoid potential disasters.

I hope you enjoy this book. I always welcome emails from readers and any feedback on how you get on with my recommendations and recipes. You can also follow me on Twitter and Instagram @MsSarahFlower. I hope you will recommend this book to others.

Happy cooking,

Sarah xx

How to use your slow cooker

Whether you are a slow cooker newbie or a seasoned pro, I would urge you to read this chapter in order to familiarise yourself with the machine and how to use it. Slow cookers are very popular for a good reason, but, depending on your machine, they can vary in style, use, temperature and cooking times, so please remember that my timings are a guide. The important factor is to get to know your machine and adapt the timings to suit.

THE BENEFITS OF SLOW COOKERS

I love slow cookers: they are not only brilliant for busy people, as they cook on a low heat, but they also maintain the nutrient value of the food. This way of cooking is also a great tool for saving money, as you can use cheaper cuts of meat that might be tougher when cooked by traditional means, but when slow cooked they produce the most delicious, tender meat. These types of meats are also much more nutrient dense, often containing more collagen, which is great for overall health, including gut health. I make my own bone stock (see page 34) in the slow cooker and it is packed with nutrients and flavour.

WHAT TO BUY?

You can buy slow cookers for as little as £15, and we are now seeing increasing popularity for multicookers, of which I am a huge fan. A multicooker is a great tool with multiple functions, hence the name. It can be used as a slow cooker, or to sauté, bake or roast, and some also have pressure cooker and even air-fryer modes.

When purchasing a slow cooker or multicooker, it is important to consider how it is going to be used. Think about the size of the machine. Some look quite big but the actual size of the crockpot might not be as big as you need. If you are cooking for a large family or you like to plan ahead and freeze food, you might be better off spending more money and investing in a larger machine. Go to an electrical store where you can actually view the machines – even if you don't buy from them – as it will give you an idea of the machines on sale and what your requirements are.

I would also strongly recommend that you buy the best you can afford. The following are the functions I absolutely love:

Multi-function As stated above, these machines are great because they combine various functions in one. The best part for me is being able to switch from sauté to slow cooker all in one machine, which is great when you want to sauté or brown off meat prior to slow cooking. This saves time and washing up (which is a win-win for me).

Timers/digital display The digital setting is great because it switches from the high or low heats to the 'keep warm' function once it has reached its set time, so you need not fear overcooking if you are late home. I feel this is absolutely vital for ensuring that your food does not spoil.

Auto Some machines have an auto button. With this function it will start off on high heat and, once the temperature has been reached, it will switch down to low. Again, this is perfect if you are out of the house, as you don't have to watch over the slow cooker.

KNOW YOUR OWN MACHINE

This is really important! Every machine is different. If you are about to purchase a machine, I would recommend buying one with a timing/digital switch as detailed above, so that it can turn itself to the warm mode once the time is reached – this saves any possible disasters with overcooking. Most have a high and low setting. If you have an old machine, check that it cooks evenly and at the expected temperature. Some can get much hotter, which can result in burning on the base or around the edges when left on high for long periods. If you are worried, use it only on low. The temperature should not create a boil – it should be a low, slow cook and not a fast, boiling cook.

MULTICOOKERS

I am a massive fan of the slow cooker and I thought I knew all there is to know about these machines. That was until I discovered the multicooker. As I've already mentioned, it has slow cooker, sauté, bake and roast functions, and some multicookers also have pressure-cooker and even air-fryer modes. Unlike most slow cookers that have lids you can see through, some multicookers have solid, pressured lids, and this means that you have no view of the food inside. Although this isn't a big problem, it does mean that you have to break the seal if you need to look at the food inside thereby reducing the heat slightly. I have also noticed when reviewing machines that some multicookers' slow-cooker functions – such as slow-cooker settings, timings and temperatures – can vary compared to standard slow cookers. Get to know your machine, as you might have to adjust the temperature or timings to suit each recipe. I love the Crock-Pot Multicooker as a simple multicooker with sauté, bake and roast functions, but my absolute favourite is the Ninja Foodi because it combines all the functions, including an air-fryer.

TO SAUTÉ OR NOT TO SAUTÉ?

Recipes often tell you to sauté the onions or brown the meat. When you brown the meat, the colour is more appealing, and it also helps to seal the meat and stops it bleeding or breaking down into the sauce. It can also increase the flavour slightly.

If you are slow cooking a whole chicken, for example, remember that this will not brown, so it might look a bit unappealing. Sautéing the chicken also stops it from flaking into the dish. Sausages are another example: I always cook (or bake) mine until they are almost cooked and golden before adding them to the slow cooker later in the dish, or if I am making a sausage casserole, I will brown them before adding. They will cook fine in the slow cooker without this, but they won't look as appetising and might not hold their shape.

All multicookers offer a sauté option and you might also find that your slow cooker has a sauté facility; others come with hob-proof dishes, allowing you to transfer from one source to the other. You will need to refer to the manufacturer's instructions for more information. Each recipe in this book will detail both techniques, allowing you to choose which you prefer.

COOKING TECHNIQUES

All slow cookers will come with full manufacturer's instructions, recipe suggestions and even a useful helpline if you get stuck. I strongly advise you to read these booklets before using your machine. Here are some reminders:

✳ Some cookers need to be preheated, which can take up to 15 minutes; others heat up fast, so you might not need to do this (refer to the manufacturer's recommendations).

✳ The recipes will occasionally have the option of cooking on high or low, depending on how quickly you need the meal. If you are not confident with your slow cooker or suspect its temperature is hotter than it should be, *always cook on low*.

✳ As a general rule of thumb, 1 hour in a conventional oven equates to 2–3 hours on high in a slow cooker, or 6 hours on low heat.

✳ Some slow cookers have an auto setting: this basically means that it heats up on high quickly, then, when it reaches temperature, it reverts to low for the remainder of the cooking time. This helps food (this is especially important with meat) to reach a safe temperature quickly.

✳ Some machines have a warm setting, which is useful if the food has reached its maximum cooking time and you are just wanting to keep it warm; however, the low setting is all that is really needed, and food can cook for 10 hours without starting to spoil.

✳ You might need to adjust the liquid content of your dish depending on your personal taste as well as the temperature of your slow cooker. The slow cooker does not evaporate liquid as much as other cooking methods, so you might need to thicken soups or casseroles cooked in it. Adding more water or stock is simple and can be done at any stage. If you find that your slow cooker does evaporate liquid, it might be overheating, so check the temperature and cook on low if you are concerned.

✳ If you have added too much liquid or the meal has become too watery (sometimes this can be due to the water content of the meat or vegetables), you can thicken it using cornflour. Simply mix a teaspoon or so of cornflour with some cold water to form a paste and add it to the liquid. It should thicken as it heats through. You can also remove the lid a little prior to serving, switch it to high and let the liquid reduce naturally.

✳ The key point to remember about slow cooking is that once you start cooking you shouldn't keep removing the lid until you are almost ready to serve. When you do this it reduces the temperature and it then takes a while for the slow cooker to return to the required heat because of the low temperature of this cooking method. The outer edge of the lid forms a seal – sometimes this might spit or bubble out, but this is quite normal. Only remove the lid when absolutely necessary – ideally just when it finishes cooking or, if necessary, in the last 30 minutes of cooking to add key ingredients. If you are the sort of person who likes to keep an eye on things, opt for a slow cooker with a glass lid (although this is not foolproof as they do get steamed up).

✳ Always defrost any frozen ingredients thoroughly before placing them in the slow cooker, especially meat. The slow cooker is designed to cook safely at low temperatures; however, if your cooker does not maintain the required heat, it could increase the risk of food poisoning caused by the spread of bacteria.

✳ Following on from the above point, if you are planning on storing the meal once cooked in the slow cooker, ensure that it has cooled completely before placing it in your containers and popping them into the fridge or freezer.

✳ When adding liquids such as stock or water, to maintain the temperature it is better to use warm liquids (not boiling) rather than cold.

SLOW COOKER PREP

Some people like to get well ahead of the game by preparing several meals and storing them in the fridge or freezer. Advance food prep can also work well with the slow cooker. Simply bag up your solid ingredients, then label, date and freeze or refrigerate them until needed. If frozen, you must defrost them before adding them to the slow cooker along with the required stock.

SLOW COOKER LINERS

These are quite a new invention but they can be useful, not just in saving washing up but they can also help to prevent food sticking to the inside of the slow cooker, so they are great when cooking items such as my toad-in-the-hole, savoury bacon and cheese bread pudding, cakes or cheesecakes. You can buy these from supermarkets, homeware stores and online.

VEGETABLES

Some vegetables, especially root vegetables, can take much longer to cook than meat. You can speed up the process by sautéing the vegetables prior to adding them to the dish, or simply chopping them into smaller chunks. Always place in the slow cooker first to ensure that they are cooked well, making sure the vegetables are thoroughly immersed in the stock, ideally on the base, as this is the hottest area.

Frozen foods such as peas, sweetcorn, spinach, mushrooms, prawns and other quick-cook foods should be added only in the last 30 minutes of cooking time.

DAIRY

Be careful when adding dairy or creamed products to the slow cooker. This should be done in the last hour or so of cooking to avoid them curdling.

FISH AND SEAFOOD

Fish tends to prefer a fast cook rather than a long cook (with the exception of squid or octopus), so it is not best suited to the slow cooker. The same applies to shellfish. If you are cooking with fish or shellfish, it might be best to add it towards the end of the cook.

CAKES AND PUDDINGS

I have made lots of cakes in the slow cooker and these have been really tasty, although sometimes they can have a different texture from oven-baked cakes. I think it is more a personal taste. I have cooked slow cooker cakes by placing batter into the slow cooker or, if you have enough space, inserting a cake dish inside the slow cooker. Or you can use two or three cake liners (this helps to hold the shape more than one) in the slow cooker. You can also use slow cooker liners and cook the cake directly in the base, but be careful if your slow cooker is old or tends to catch in areas. As a precaution, always cook on low. You can also use individual ramekin dishes; if this is the case, you will need to reduce the cooking time by half.

The slow cooker can sometimes get quite wet inside because of the condensation and steam produced during the cook. It is simple to prevent this by putting a tea towel over the top of the open slow cooker before adding the lid. Full details will be given with each recipe and on page 204.

When cooking some desserts, you can add water to the base to create a bain-marie (a water bath), which works well with some sponge puddings or cheesecakes.

PUDDING BASINS
See page 204 for instructions of how to get a pudding basin in and out of the slow cooker easily.

HERBS AND SPICES

The slow cooker is designed for long, low-heat cooking. Fresh herbs would lose their flavour, so it is always best to use dried herbs or, if you like to use fresh, add them in the last 1 hour–30 minutes of cooking time. I like to use spices in some recipes, especially chilli. Fresh chilli is fine to use, but remember that a long, slow cook for chilli can increase the intensity of the chilli, so you might want to adjust to taste.

PASTA

Most slow cooker recipes using pasta will ask you to add this, already cooked, towards the end of the cooking time. This is because pasta is quite delicate and can break down if you cook it for long periods. The exception is my macaroni cheese, found on page 163, which is a shorter cook where you can throw it all in at once.

How to feed your family for less

It does not matter if you are aiming to save money or live a healthy lifestyle, or both: you will still need to learn to be a savvy shopper. Most people walk around supermarkets in a trance-like state, picking up items from habit rather than need or desire. As a nutritionist, I often hear people state that healthy food is more expensive, but really that is not always true. Healthy food is real food. Cooking from scratch can save you pounds, but it can also dramatically improve your health. The slow cooker is a great tool, because it helps you to create healthy meals from scratch with the minimum of fuss. You can also double up recipes to create your own convenient ready meals.

BE PREPARED

Always, always, always make a list before shopping, planning your meals before you set off. This will help keep you focused and less likely to buy unwanted or doubled-up items. I cannot emphasise this enough. You can save pounds every week by being organised and following your list. If you only take one thing from this book, please let it be the power of list making! If all that seems like hard work, you can shop online. The beauty of this is that those magic gremlins actually store your information, so when you place your next order, you will be able to check on your favourites; you will have an automatic list, plus you are less likely to overspend online as you are not being tempted by foods you don't want or need.

BUY WITH YOUR HEAD, NOT YOUR STOMACH

Never go grocery shopping when you are hungry. It is a sure-fire way to spend more money. You will get to the checkout and discover your trolley is heaving with crisps, chocolate and biscuits.

BOGOF DEALS

'Buy one get one free' can seem like a great deal, but only if you were intending to buy the product in the first place. Sadly, most of these amazing offers are for the unhealthiest foods, so proceed with caution. Before you buy, remember to compare the price.

You might find that you are paying more than double when compared to other brands. Don't be fooled into thinking that the manufacturers or supermarkets are offering a free item out of the goodness of their hearts. It is purely a marketing tool to lure us into buying products we might not normally buy, or to help launch a new range. The golden rule is: only buy if it saves you money, it is something you need and something you will use.

If the item is something you use on a weekly basis, it is worth looking at. Fresh items will not last long, but you might be able to freeze them. Consider carefully how this will fit into your weekly or monthly menu plans before buying.

DITCH THE BRANDS

Moving away from the brands doesn't always mean jumping from a premium brand straight to a no-frills product; you can look at the middle-of-the-range products on the shelf. I have noticed no difference in quality for a number of value items – such as dried pasta, flour, butter and even some biscuits. It is all down to personal taste. Also, think about supermarkets such as Aldi or Lidl, that have some amazing own brands that are almost identical to a leading brand. For fresh fruit and veg, I really like wonky veg – who cares if a carrot is slightly wonky?

WASTE NOT, WANT NOT

Families do waste a lot of food. According to a study by Waste and Resources Action Programme (WRAP) in January 2020, UK households waste 4.5m tonnes of food a year that could have been eaten, worth £14bn. This amounts to £700 for an average family with children. That is a huge amount of money just thrown into the bin. We either waste because we have cooked too much or we waste because we have let the food go off. Some people throw things out because they are scared of use-by/best-before dates. We have forgotten to look at the food, not just the date! Keeping track of what is in your fridge is key. Anything nearing a use by date needs to be either used or, if it can be, frozen. The best-before date is just a guide, so use your judgement. Apples are a case in point here. Traditionally, apples would have been picked in the early autumn and stored in a cool place to last the rest of the year. I buy apples and store them in my fridge. They can be perfect for a few months past their best-before date stored this way.

BE STORE-CUPBOARD SAVVY

Try to keep your store-cupboard stocked with a variety of canned, dried and frozen goods that you know your family love to eat. Tinned beans and tomatoes, frozen vegetables, meat and fish, pasta, noodles, rice and grains are all everyday essentials with a long shelf life – meaning that you will always have the ingredients standing by to pull together a delicious meal or to jazz up your leftovers.

PLAN AHEAD AND STORE WELL TO AVOID WASTE

The main foods we waste are fruit, cheese, vegetables and meat. All of which can be frozen or used if you plan ahead. Get into the habit of planning meals in advance, thinking about what you have in the fridge, and keep an eye on what needs to be used first.

Extend the life of your more perishable foods. There are lots of amazing products available which really do extend the life of your food.

✳ Vacuum packers are great as they remove the air and can extend the life of a food 3–5 times longer than placing it in plastic containers or bags.

✳ You can buy bags for potatoes, vegetables or even bananas that create the best environment to extend the life of the food.

✳ You can buy gadgets including discs or pads, to place in your fridge or fruit bowl, which help absorb ethylene gas – the chemical emitted by fruit and vegetables as they ripen – which in turn speeds up the decaying process of the foods. My favourite is the fruit and veg saver discs and Lakeland's fruit and veg cushion.

✳ If you are fed up with your cheese going off quickly, invest in something like the Tefal cheese preserver, which has a replaceable filter to help prevent odours as well as to regulate humidity.

Think about using up all your vegetables or freezing what you don't use. If I have an excess of fresh vegetables or I know they need using up quickly, I either make something with them, such as a soup or casserole, and freeze this as a spare meal, or I chop and store, ready to defrost and cook with later on. Leeks, onions, peppers, garlic, chillies and swede are common things I chop and pop in the freezer ready to pull out and use as and when needed. Fresh tomatoes can make wonderful pasta sauces. Soft broccoli can make a fabulous broccoli and Stilton soup.

If you plan ahead with menu plans you should have very little waste. Think about your meals; for example, if you are making mashed potato for one meal, double up and use it for the next night as a topping for shepherd's pie. Making pastry? Double up and store in the fridge or freeze it ready for your next baking session. Alternatively, make some pastry cases and freeze them ready to add your filling.

LOVE YOUR LEFTOVERS

It's amazing how many meals you can get from one chicken! How many of us have a roast chicken but after carving it we simply throw the carcass away? This carcass will often have enough meat left on the bone and underneath to fill a pie or make a quick curry. If you enjoy a roast on Sunday, the remains of the joint would make a delicious risotto later in the week and you'll always find enough for a sandwich. It is often not that much more expensive to buy a larger chicken or joint, but it could give you an additional meal or two. You can also use your slow cooker to make a delicious stock from the leftover carcass for using in soups or other dishes (see page 35).

Use your store-cupboard essentials to create meals from leftovers, bulking up meals with beans or pulses. Rice would turn leftover chicken into a lovely chicken biryani (see page 182). With leftover meat from your roast you can use a mincer to make your own minced meat. Add a tin of lentils to your minced meat to make it stretch further.

....

LEFTOVERS	IDEAS TO AVOID WASTE
Mashed potato	Use as a topping for meals such as shepherd's pie, make into cheese-and-onion pasties, potato croquettes, fish cakes, bubble and squeak
Pastry	Transfer to another dish, make pastry cases ready to use (these can be frozen), freeze pastry in a freezer bag or keep refrigerated for 3 days.
Joints of meat or chicken after a roast	Turn into curry, stir-fry, pies, casseroles, soups or pasties. There really are endless ways to use up meat and poultry, so don't throw it away. If you are aware of the use-by dates, you should be able to transfer the uncooked meat to the freezer if you know you won't use it in time. Always follow the correct health-and-safety advice when handling and freezing meat and poultry.
Vegetables	When vegetables need using up you can make delicious soups or casseroles, or freeze them. I freeze all veg – chopped onions, peppers, diced root veg – then I just pull out handfuls when I need them to add to a recipe.
Cooked vegetables	You can turn these into a quick soup or make a more traditional bubble and squeak. Leftover cooked potatoes can be turned into a multitude of meals: my favourite dish using leftover boiled or new potatoes is homity pie.
Fruit	Don't waste fruit! You can freeze fruits such as banana, kiwi, berries, mango, melon, etc. They're perfect to use in smoothies. Frozen banana can also be used to make banana cake. I have placed frozen banana slices in an ovenproof dish and covered them with custard for a quick-and-easy pudding. Apples, pears, plums and rhubarb can be frozen or made into delicious crumbles or pies.

Herbs	If you have fresh herbs that need using up, you can mix with some olive oil and save in ice cube trays to freeze. These are great to use as a herby base oil for sautéing. Alternatively, mix the fresh herbs with butter. You can pop this into ice-cube trays as above or form the butter into a sausage, cut into discs and freeze. These can be used to add to baked fish or when you are sautéing.
Custard	Whether you make your own or buy ready-made, sometimes you have half a jug of custard left. Add some fruit and turn it into ice lollies for the children.
Eggs	Some recipes ask for only an egg yolk to be used. When this happens, I pop the egg white into freezer bags and label how many egg whites it contains. I then use this to make meringues.
Tomatoes	Never throw these away! I am a big fan of roasting tomatoes in garlic and herbs – I then use this as a base for a pasta sauce, topping for pizza or to add to a casserole or any dish that uses tomatoes. You can place the roasted tomatoes in a sterilised jar and keep them in the fridge for up to one week.
Bread	Don't throw this away; whizz it in your food processor to make breadcrumbs. You can also freeze slices of bread ready to make bread-and-butter pudding or even summer pudding. This also works well with fruit bread or buns. (See also page 18 for more about breadcrumbs.)
Milk	Milk that needs using up can be frozen, or why not make something like a rice pudding, custard, white sauce or cheese sauce? Anything that you use regularly can be made and frozen.
Crisps	Have you got a squashed packed of crisps or leftover tortilla crisps? Use them for a crispy topping on a savoury dish or even crushed to make a crispy coating for your homemade fish fingers.
Cereal	Do you have leftover cereal in the bottom of the packet but not enough to fill a bowl? My children love to mix and match, so we have a container where the cereal gets mixed up. You can also use leftover cereal in cakes, crumbles (as a topping) or toppings for savoury dishes (cornflakes work brilliantly for this).

Make use of your freezer

Years ago people bought large chest freezers in a bid to save as much time and money as possible. Over the last 30 years, we have seen a decline in the need for these large freezers as more and more families opted for fresh food, processed food and takeaways, although the onset of COVID-19 in early 2020 saw a surge in sales of freezers, as people wanted to store more food. We are, however, still seeing a huge amount of food waste. Using a bit of savvy and a more frugal head, you can make the most of your freezer, fridge and store-cupboard, avoid waste, save time and, most importantly for the readers of this book, save money.

If you are planning to save money, a freezer is a great asset. You can fill this with bargains, food grown from your allotment (if you have one) and with homemade ready meals. Freezers work more efficiently when used fully, so fill it up but make a note of what is going in. If you are adding home-produced meals, label each with the contents and the date you put it in the freezer. Remember, the bigger the freezer, the easier it is to lose track of the contents. If buying a new one, make sure you buy one with the best energy-efficiency grading.

Opinion is split on the nutritional value of frozen food. I believe that it is all about balance, and I like to look at the bigger picture. Most busy families rely heavily on processed or take-away food. For them, opting instead to utilise a freezer packed with freshly frozen homemade food is by far the better and healthier option. A freezer is also, over the long term, better for the environment because you are creating less waste – plus, as reiterated in these opening chapters, it can save you money.

THE BIG FREEZE

If you need to replace your fridge or freezer, make sure you opt for the most energy-efficient one. A-grade fridges will save you approximately £35 a year compared to less efficient models.

To help your fridge or freezer run more efficiently:

✳ Defrost your fridge and freezer regularly.

✳ Keep your fridge and freezer at least three-quarters full. If you have a large chest freezer and cannot fill it with food, add cardboard boxes or rolled-up newspaper to help to fill it up.

✳ Do not leave the fridge or freezer door open longer than necessary.

✳ Make sure that the door seals are working correctly.

✳ Do not place warm or hot food into the fridge or freezer – allow the food to cool first.

✳ Keep air circulating around the fridge or freezer, particularly around the condenser coils at the back. Clear the condensers of dust regularly, as dust can reduce efficiency by up to 25 per cent.

GET PREPARED

Start saving your old containers. You can use margarine and butter containers, small milk cartons, yoghurt pots and ice-cube trays (preferably silicon as the ice cubes pop out easier). I have sets of BPA-free plastic containers and I also use freezer bags. I love the Stasher Reusable bags, but also use ones from Lakeland specifically for liquids (Soup 'n' Sauce). I tend to buy freezer bags with Ziplock seals, as these make life so much easier.

Always remember to label and date items that you are placing in the fridge or freezer, and, ideally, plan when you are going to use them. You really don't want to have bits and pieces of food in your freezer for longer than a few months.

HERBS

If you love cooking, you probably buy fresh herbs. These are great if you can grow them in pots or in the garden, but if you are buying fresh from the supermarket, you might be paying a premium. If you can't grow your own, or it is the wrong time of the year, one great product I have recently tried is frozen herbs. For the same price as fresh, you can buy a large container of freshly frozen herbs that can last you months and offer a superior taste over the dried variety. Simply use what you want and pop the rest back into the freezer. If you grow your own and have a surplus, you can freeze herbs yourself. Some herbs go limp when frozen but will still maintain their flavour. Herbs that freeze well are basil, coriander, oregano, sage, dill, rosemary, mint, lemongrass, chives, tarragon and thyme. I also freeze fresh chillies, garlic and ginger.

FREEZE TO AVOID WASTE

It is really frustrating to throw away half-empty jars, tubes, tins or loaves of bread. Well, now you don't have to. Here are some tips to make the most of those odds and ends that we all usually discard around the kitchen. (See also the list of uses for leftovers on page 14.)

Bread Stale or leftover bread can be turned into breadcrumbs. Spread them out on a baking tray (to avoid them clumping together), freeze and put into a container or freezer bag. French sticks or speciality breads and bread rolls can go stale very quickly. Freeze them and, when defrosted ready for eating, revitalise them with a few splashes of water, then bake in the oven at 180°C/160°C fan oven/Gas 4 for 2–3 minutes.

Cheese You can grate cheese and, as for breadcrumbs above, put it on a tray to avoid it clumping together, then freeze before transferring it to a container or freezer bag. This is an ideal tip for leftover cheeses, especially those that we might not buy very often, such as blue cheese. It's great for Parmesan, as it lasts for a very long time and it avoids the smelly fridge scenario.

Pesto, pastes and purées If, like me, you love spicy pastes and herb purées or pesto, put any leftovers in silicon ice-cube trays. These are easy to pop out in portion-sized dollops and it avoids you finding mouldy jars at the back of your fridge. You can also use this tip to freeze herb butters.

Ripe avocados can have the flesh scooped out and mixed with a touch of lemon or lime juice before being frozen. Once defrosted, use to make tasty dips.

Nuts and seeds I use a lot of nuts and seeds in my food and store them in airtight jars, but if I buy them in bulk, they can be frozen, which can prevent them from becoming stale.

Sweet potato/squash/pumpkin I sometimes have pieces of these in my vegetable tray that need using up. To avoid waste, I chop up usable chunks, coat them with lemon juice to prevent discolouration, and put them in a freezer bag to freeze. They are ideal for adding to casseroles when I don't have any fresh to hand.

Lemons Sometimes recipes ask you for the zest and juice of half a lemon. You can squeeze the lemon juice from the remaining half and place it in an ice-cube tray and freeze it until needed. A friend of mine slices lemons into wedges, freezes them and uses them in her gin and tonic – she says it saves on adding ice!

Pastry Ready-made shop-bought pastry does not have to be the only pastry in your freezer. Why not double up your batch of homemade pastry and place the leftovers in the freezer for another day? Alternatively, think of some extra ways to use the pastry up: you could make mini tarts or pies and put them in the freezer ready to cook and serve as delicious nibbles for an impromptu drinks party, or cooked and ready to use in your packed lunch.

Mashed potato Have you overestimated your mashed potato? Why not freeze it in little portion sizes? It's ideal to reheat when in a hurry or to use as a topping or even to make into a fish cake.

Peppers/chillies/garlic/onions Chop and place in a freezer bag until needed.

Swede/turnip/celeriac/parsnip Sometimes a swede, turnip or celeriac can be too large for your immediate needs. Slice the unwanted swede or turnip into chunks and put it in the freezer until needed. You can also do this with celeriac. I make celeriac roasts, so I cut the celeriac into roast-potato-sized chunks ready to cook. Parsnips can also be cut into lengths ready to roast or chop into a casserole.

Bananas I was always throwing away brown bananas in our house as my boys are really fussy with bruised fruit. I try to use up what I can in smoothies, but I still had the odd bit of waste. I now use a banana bag from Lakeland and it works really well. I have also tried freezing bananas – great for smoothies or banana cake. I simply slice it into a container and use as and when needed.

Curry, casseroles or pasta sauces Leftover curry, casserole or pasta sauces can be frozen ready to be transformed into a new dish later on. You can also prepare your own curry sauce, double the recipe and freeze half ready for another meal.

Ripe tomatoes can be chopped and frozen ready to use in tomato or pasta sauces in place of tinned chopped tomatoes. I also like to slow bake them in the oven with garlic and herbs then put them in jars with some olive oil.

Berries I absolutely love berries. My freezer is always well stocked with a variety of fruit berries ready for smoothies or delicious deserts. To freeze your own berries, put on a baking try so that they are not touching each other, and freeze. Once frozen, you can scoop them up and put them in a freezer bag or container.

Vegetables You can freeze most vegetables. Although vegetables are traditionally blanched (plunged in a pan of boiling water for 3 minutes) before they are frozen, I simply freeze them. If I want to freeze broccoli or cauliflower, for example, I cut them into florets, put them on a baking tray to prevent the florets from sticking to each other, freeze then transfer them to a bag. Alternatively, you can make a delicious soup or casserole with any leftover vegetables, then freeze it to make a nutritious homemade ready meal.

Pulses (peas, beans and lentils) are great and you can store them in their dried form for months. I have lots of glass Kilner jars in my kitchen and a pantry filled with a variety of pulses; however, cooking them can be a bit of a faff. You can, of course, buy canned, but this does cost a little more in the long run. Instead, why not bulk cook and then freeze, ready to add to your favourite recipe?

Wine If you have any wine left in the bottom of a bottle, you can freeze it in small portions ready to add to casseroles or pasta sauces. I use wine in a lot of my casseroles, but I do tend to buy the cheapest wine for cooking purposes only.

Tortilla wraps My eldest son is the only one who loves wraps, so one bag of ten inevitably ends up with wraps wasted. I freeze the wraps, ensuring that there is baking parchment between each wrap. He defrosts them for 20–30 seconds in the microwave before filling them to his heart's content.

Lollipop, lollipop Kids (and adults) love lollipops and ice creams. I have some silicon ice-cream moulds, which are easy to fill and form the perfect twirled ice lollies. Fill these with leftover juices, smoothies or even custard.

Bake one, bake one free My mum would never use the oven unless you could fill it up. If you are baking or being creative in the kitchen, why not double up and make more? You can then freeze one, saving you time, energy and money. This is great for everyone, whether you are a single person or a family of four – as long as you have freezer space, you can save time and money.

✳ When baking with pastry, I always double up the recipes and place one uncooked pie or pastry tart in the freezer. Christmas is a great time to get ahead with a whole host of savoury and sweet pastry delights, making the most of your puff, filo and shortcrust pastry.

✳ Cakes and biscuits also freeze well. If you are freezing a decorated cake or gateau, freeze it unwrapped, then put into a freezer bag or container to avoid damaging the decoration.

Double up Don't just freeze items for baking; you can also freeze complete meals, so learn to double up your recipes. Meat, fish, poultry and vegetarian meals can all be frozen, although be aware of the correct reheating and defrosting procedures with meat, poultry and fish. Remember always to label and date your foods. When parboiling potatoes ready to roast, you can double up and place unwanted pieces in the freezer until ready to use another day. Simply defrost gently, coat with your oil/paprika mix and roast in the preheated oven. Some people coat the potatoes in the oil or herb mixture before freezing them.

Store-cupboard essentials

When we are talking about budget cooking, we need some key essentials. I am a very simple, traditional cook. I use everyday ingredients and I always have the basics, which are replaced regularly. I also keep a good stock of store-cupboard foods and basic vegetables such as onions, garlic, carrots, potatoes, and so on. You will find your own favourites, but here is my list.

FRESH VEGETABLES AND FLAVOURINGS

It's always best to buy your fruit and vegetables when they are in season. This not only makes them cheaper, but also they will be much tastier and more nutrient dense because they are fresh from the field to the plate. If you are lucky to live near a farmers' market, visit this regularly and you can pick up some amazing bargains. Also look out for great deals in supermarkets such as Aldi's 'Super 6', Morrison's 'Wonky Veg' and other weekly fruit-and-vegetable deals to save money.

You might notice that swede is not on the list of ingredients below. This is because swede can be quite overpowering when added to a casserole, so I tend to use it as a mash or a vegetable accompaniment rather than adding it to my slow cooker dishes.

Carrots These are cheap and they help to bulk out casseroles and stews. They are also great as a side vegetable.

Celery adds flavour to some casseroles. You can also make a wonderful soup with celery – see my Celery and Stilton Soup on page 47.

Chilli I do love fresh chilli, but you can opt for chilli paste or chilli in a jar if you don't have any fresh. You can also use frozen chillies. Fresh chillies give a different flavour from chilli powder, so these are not interchangeable.

Garlic I use garlic in lots of dishes, so there's always some fresh in my house; however, you can also buy garlic chopped in jars, as a paste or frozen.

Ginger I am a big fan of fresh ginger as it can really lift a meal. You will find it in the vegetable aisle of the supermarket.

If I have any fresh ginger that needs using up, I slice it thinly and place in a jar and top it up with white wine vinegar; or you can chop it and freeze.

Green vegetables These are more for your side dishes rather than to be cooked in the slow cooker. Steamed green vegetables go with most dishes. Some recipes ask for spinach, but you can substitute it with kale, chard or even green cabbage.

Mushrooms are wonderful for adding flavour. I always store my mushrooms in a paper bag or a mushroom bag, because the plastic containers they come in from the supermarket produce more moisture and this can shorten their shelf life.

Onions are vital for most savoury recipes as a way of adding flavour. I love using red onions, as they have an amazing colour and can have a milder flavour.

Parsnips When in season these are great to add to a casserole.

Peppers I always have a selection of red, yellow and green peppers in my fridge because they are very versatile and a tasty addition to many dishes.

Potatoes and sweet potato I always like to have large and new potatoes around, and I store them in the fridge. You can buy potato sacks from Lakeland, which help to extend the life of the potato. Sweet potato is also great for adding to slow cookers as well as for roasting or making chunky chips.

Spinach I use baby leaf spinach, but if you don't have fresh you can use a few blocks of frozen spinach. As stated above, you can also use other green vegetables if you don't have spinach. Chard and kale are the best swaps.

Squash/pumpkin There are a few recipes in this book that use squash or pumpkin – both are interchangeable. If you don't have squash, you could use sweet potato.

DRIED HERBS AND SPICES

For slow-cooker meals, you should always have a good selection of dried herbs and spices; don't waste your money on fresh herbs when using the slow cooker, because, as noted earlier, the long cooking times weaken their flavours, unless they are added in the last half hour of cooking. You don't have to go mad and buy the entire shelf of herbs and spices. The following is a list of items used in this book. I buy from a local warehouse or my co-operative where they sell 500g bags for less than I would pay for one small pot in the supermarket.

Basil is quite potent, so a little goes a long way. It's great for Mediterranean-style meals.

Cayenne pepper adds some heat to spicy dishes.

Chilli powder or freeze-dried chillies are useful for adding a bit of spice to your dishes. I have both mild and hot in my store-cupboard to help me build flavour. I also grow my own chilli plants in the summer. Any leftover chillies I bottle in oil or freeze whole until I need them.

Cumin I use this in my homemade curry pastes.

Curry powder This is a blend of herbs and spices traditionally used in Indian cookery, such as garam masala, tikka masala or standard curry powder. If you are unsure, opt for a medium curry powder.

Dried bay leaves Don't underestimate a bay leaf – it can really lift a savoury dish, particularly soups. Ask around your friends to see if anyone has a bay tree; they might let you have some leaves to dry out and store but they're also easy to buy.

Ground cinnamon I love cinnamon, especially in biscuits, apple cakes or apple pies, but I also use it in curries and tagines.

Ground coriander is lovely in savoury dishes, but I also use it in cakes, as it has a surprising flavour.

Ground ginger Don't mistake this for fresh ginger, as the tastes are quite different. Ground ginger is good in savoury dishes and is excellent for baking.

Ground turmeric Some call this the poor man's saffron, and you have probably heard of its use as an anti-inflammatory due to its active component curcumin. Add it to savoury dishes or use it to colour rice that lovely vibrant yellow.

Mixed/Italian herbs This is a safe option for newbie cooks. Add to savoury dishes, salad dressings and even sprinkle on pizzas if you don't have any oregano.

Mixed spice is optional but good if you love baking.

Nutmeg I keep a few whole nutmegs in a jar and use a fine grater to add a bit of nutmeg magic to my food. It's great used in baking, but also very comforting sprinkled on milky drinks and puddings.

Oregano I tend to use this a lot, because I love Mediterranean-style food.

Marjoram I use this in cottage pies or chillies. It has a more delicate flavour than oregano.

Mustard Wholegrain mustard works well in dishes such as my pork tenderloin recipe (page 97) and I use Dijon mustard in my Chilli-Infused Beef Stroganoff (page 72). I also use mustard powder occasionally to add flavour. One teaspoon works well in a cheese sauce – you could consider adding this for extra punch in the macaroni cheese recipe on page 163.

Paprika This rich, red spice has a very delicate flavour. I use it on my roast potatoes and also in soups and casseroles – even sprinkled on cheese on toast. I find paprika goes very well with beef, enhancing the flavour, so you will often find this combination. I also like to use smoked paprika in some dishes as well as in a chilli or my Spiced Chorizo and Chickpea Pot (page 101).

Parsley is another popular herb to add some flavour and colour to a dish.

Ras el hanout is a blend of spices, typically from North Africa. I use this in a few recipes in this book, such as my Spiced Lamb Meatballs with Couscous (page 119) and my Moroccan Vegetable One Pot (page 172).

Rosemary I don't use a lot of rosemary, but sometimes it can really help to lift the flavour of a dish.

Star anise This is optional in a couple of recipes but it does add a lovely aniseed flavour when used.

Tarragon This is a lovely herb, and it goes really well with chicken or fish.

Thyme goes especially well with chicken and pork. It's one of my favourite herbs.

STORE-CUPBOARD BASICS USED IN THE RECIPES

This list is my go-to store-cupboard essentials. Stocked well, it can help to transform meals and create delicious desserts with ease.

Cocoa and chocolate chips are used in the book, and plain chocolate also is great for adding to desserts and cakes.

Coconut cream is available from supermarkets and is usually found in cardboard containers near the spices aisle. Do not confuse this with creamed coconut, which is a different product.

Cornflour is a useful ingredient to help thicken sauces. It is easy to use: just mix it with a little water before adding it to the mixture in the slow cooker.

Dried fruit Mixed dried fruit is essential if you love baking cakes or biscuits. I also add a sprinkle to apple pies. You can even add a few sultanas to create a sweet curry sauce.

Flour – plain and self-raising You can buy flour for less than 30p a bag (own brands). It is used for baking, making pastry, desserts, dumplings and thickening sauces.

Olive oil Buy the best quality you can afford as not all olive oil is equal. Some are blends of other oils. You do not need to use extra virgin in the slow cooker or for sautéing (leave that for good salad dressings). You only need small amounts when cooking, so a little goes a long way. I also use sesame oil in my Sweet-and-Sour Pork (page 181), but you can omit this if you do not have it.

Olives You can buy olives in jars or fresh. A few of my Mediterranean recipes use olives, but you can omit them if you prefer.

Pasta This has become a family essential; it's cheap and cheerful, but nutritionally it is always better to opt for wholewheat varieties. You can also buy gluten-free and wheat-free versions including spelt, vegetable, bean, rice and corn pasta. Don't forget that you can make your own vegetable pasta if you have a spiraliser – it's a good way to use up leftover courgettes!

Red lentils If you are new to pulses, red lentils are perfect because they don't need to be soaked. You can use them in soups, casseroles and even rice dishes. They also make a tasty dhal.

Rice is popular with many people. My personal preference is brown basmati for my family, but I tend to eat more low-carb options such as cauliflower rice now (see page 185).

Soy sauce is used in dishes such as my Sweet-and-Sour Pork (page 186).

Stock cubes I make my own stock, but I also occasionally use a stock cube. I like to use the gel stock cubes, but that is a personal preference. You can get stock cubes in most meat flavours and you can also get vegetable and even red wine stock cubes.

Sugar You can always bake something if you have flour, eggs, butter and sugar.

Suet This is great for suet puddings but also dumplings. See my recipe for Beef Stew and Dumplings (page 83). You can buy this as beef suet or vegetarian suet: both are fine to use.

Sweetcorn is useful to add to dishes such as my Brunswick-Style Stew on page 139. Buy it either in tins or frozen.

Tinned beans Beans – either cannellini, chickpeas, butter beans, kidney beans or even mixed beans – are great to have in your store-cupboard and I use them frequently in this book. Tinned are cheap and easy to use. Dried work out cheaper in the long run but they have to be cooked well before using. This book uses kidney beans, white beans, cannellini beans, butter beans and mixed beans.

Tinned tomatoes Tinned tomatoes are a fraction of the price of fresh tomatoes and work very well in the slow cooker. I buy chopped tomatoes. Sun-dried tomatoes are also great to have on standby – adding a few pieces to a tomato soup enhances its flavour.

Tomato purée You can buy tubes or tins of tomato purée for less than 30p. I prefer tubes. I also use sun-dried tomato paste for a deeper flavour, but if you don't have this, you can swap it with traditional tomato purée.

Wine I like to use wine in my casseroles to add depth of flavour. If you prefer not to use this, you can use stock instead. When using wine in cooking, I tend to opt for whatever cheap option I can find. I also use rice wine vinegar or white wine vinegar in one dish – my Sweet-and-Sour Pork on page 186.

Worcester sauce is a robust sauce for adding flavour, especially to meaty dishes such as my Loaded Cottage Pie (page 71).

Yeast extract (such as Marmite) adds flavour to your dishes, and it's also useful to create a meaty flavour in vegetarian or vegan dishes.

FRIDGE STORE

Your fridge houses your fresh ingredients, so these will need to be replaced regularly. Here is a list of the essentials I tend to have in my fridge all the time.

Butter is essential for cooking and baking. I'm not a fan of margarine, due to its processed and inflammatory properties, but I have given the option for both in my dessert chapters.

Cheese I buy mature Cheddar, especially for cooking, because you don't need to use as much of it as you would milder Cheddars and other cheeses. I also regularly use mozzarella, goat's cheese, ricotta and Parmesan.

Cooking bacon is excellent for adding flavour, but don't buy expensive diced pancetta; you can buy cooking bacon, which comes in thick rashers, and dice it – it works just as well as pancetta and brings a wonderful flavour for half the price.

Cream makes creamy sauces and soups. I use double cream in my recipes.

Cream cheese Add it to dishes in the slow cooker to create a lovely creamy sauce. You can also use it to make a quick-and-easy mousse, a cheesecake and even a simple cheese sauce. I always buy full-fat cream cheese, as I find the low-fat products are more prone to separating when cooking.

Crème fraîche can be used in cooking in the same way as cream cheese and instead of cream.

Eggs You can always make a meal with an egg! They are great for cooking, baking and snacks.

Milk I use full-fat milk for cooking as it adds more richness and tends not to separate. If you don't use whole milk, you can store it in the freezer to use for cooking. You can divide it up into smaller quantities before freezing, if you like.

Natural yoghurt I buy Greek yoghurt; it can be used in cooking because it is thick and it holds well when cooked; it also lovely as a dessert topping.

FREEZER STORE

As I have explained, I use my freezer a lot but mainly for storing my homemade meals or adding any leftover vegetables or meat. See the 'Make use of your freezer' (page 16) for more advice.

Peas and other vegetables are useful as a standby but remember that fresh is better than frozen, so try to include some fresh for your five a day!

Puff pastry I always have some puff pastry on standby; it is used in my Steak and Ale Pie recipe (page 79) and my Chicken and Mushroom Pie (page 143).

CONVERSION CHARTS

WEIGHT		LIQUIDS			MEASUREMENTS	
Metric	Imperial	Metric	Imperial	US cup	Metric	Imperial
25g	1oz	5ml	1 tsp	1 tsp	5cm	2in
50g	2oz	15ml	1 tbsp	1 tbsp	10cm	4in
75g	3oz	50ml	2fl oz	3 tbsp	13cm	5in
100g	4oz	60ml	2½fl oz	¼ cup	15cm	6in
150g	5oz	75ml	3fl oz	⅓ cup	18cm	7in
175g	6oz	100ml	4fl oz	scant ½ cup	20cm	8in
200g	7oz	125ml	4½fl oz	½ cup	25cm	10in
225g	8oz	150ml	5fl oz	⅔ cup	30cm	12in
250g	9oz	200ml	7fl oz	scant 1 cup		
300g	10oz	250ml	9fl oz	1 cup		
350g	12oz	300ml	½ pint	1¼ cups		
400g	14oz	350ml	12fl oz	1⅓ cups		
450g	1lb	400ml	¾ pint	1¾ cups		
		500ml	17fl oz	2 cups		
		600ml	1 pt	2½ cups		

SYMBOLS

Double up & freeze

Vegetarian

Vegan

Dairy free option

1

Bursting with nutrients, and quick and easy to make, soups can make a healthy snack or a nutritious meal. They are a great way to add extra vegetables to your family's diet. They are also cheap to make and very filling. Best of all, as they are slow cooked at a low temperature, the nutrients are maintained, making the soup ultra-healthy.

If you or your child has a packed lunch, why not invest in a small flask and fill it with your homemade soup? It's perfect to fill up and warm the body, especially during the winter months. Most soups can be frozen, so fill your freezer with individual portions ready for lunches.

SOUP-MAKING ADVICE

Stock Stock cubes can be quite overpowering and also high in salt and sugar, but there are some great products available these days that give a more natural flavour. I use my own stock, but I also really like using gel stocks for added flavour. Homemade stock is packed with nutrients, particularly if you use animal bones. You can freeze this stock, so make it in larger quantities and freeze it in batches. Bought stock can be rather salty, so always be careful when adding salt to a recipe using bought stock.

. . . .

HOMEMADE STOCKS

BONE BROTH (MAKES 2–3 LITRES)

If you are using meaty bones, you can roast them first to help release the flavours and nutrients, although this step isn't absolutely necessary. Preheat the oven to 180°C (160°C fan oven) Gas 4, then roast 1kg bones (bone marrow, ribs, knuckles) for 45 minutes.

Preheat your slow cooker, following the manufacturer's instructions. Put the bones in the slow cooker and add 100ml apple cider vinegar and 2 quartered large onions. Roughly chop 2 garlic cloves, 2 carrots (optional) and 3 celery sticks, and add to the bones. Add 2 tsp dried mixed herbs, a small handful of fresh parsley (or 2 tsp dried), 2 bay leaves and 2 tsp black peppercorns, then cover with water.

Cook on low for 24 hours (for bones that have been roasted) or up to 48 hours for raw bones. Remove any scum from the surface of the water (this is perfectly normal) using a slotted spoon. When cooked, remove the crock from the slow cooker and carefully strain the broth. Leave it to cool and settle; it will form a layer of fat on the top once cooled but you can scrape this off and use it as cooking fat. Transfer to a container to keep in the fridge, or portion into freezer bags or ice-cube trays to freeze.

CHICKEN BROTH (SERVES 4)

Preheat your slow cooker, following the manufacturer's instructions. Put 1 chicken carcass into the slow cooker and add 1 large quartered onion. Roughly chop 1 carrot and 3 celery sticks, and add to the carcass. Add 2 tsp dried thyme, a small handful of fresh parsley (or 2 tsp dried), 2 bay leaves and 2 tsp black peppercorns, then cover with water. Cook on low for 12–24 hours (longer cooking will produce a richer stock).

When cooked, remove the crock from the slow cooker and carefully strain the broth through a sieve (to make sure you remove any tiny bones). Transfer to a container to keep in the fridge, or portion into freezer bags or ice-cube trays to freeze.

. . . .

Puréeing soups Some people like a chunky soup; others prefer a smooth soup. It is purely personal taste. When puréeing a soup I use an electric hand blender (also called a stick blender). It is simple to use and saves on washing up and the messy transfer to a liquidiser and back again (although make sure that the end of the blender is fully submerged in the soup or you will end up with it everywhere). For a really fine soup, you can strain it through a sieve.

Chunky soups Some chunky soups benefit from a thicker stock or sauce. To do this, simply remove about a quarter of the soup and blend it, then add it back to the soup.

Liquid – thick or thin? You might need to adjust the liquid content of your soup depending on your personal taste. The slow cooker does not evaporate liquid as readily as other cooking methods, so you might need to thicken the soups. (See page 6 for my advice on using your slow cooker and adjusting the heats.)

Here are my top tips to thicken soups or casseroles

✳ You can remove the lid of the slow cooker and allow the steam to evaporate, which helps to reduce the liquid.

✳ Mix a couple of teaspoons of cornflour with cold water, pour into the mixture in the slow cooker and stir well.

✳ Remove some of the chunky soup and purée it before mixing it back in the slow-cooker mixture.

✳ Add a handful of red lentils and cook on high for 30 minutes.

Pulses and beans Adding pulses (peas, beans and lentils) is a cheap way to bulk out a meal, and it also adds essential nutrients to your dish and can keep you feeling fuller for longer.

Creams Creams, milk, Greek yoghurt and crème fraîche can sometimes separate when cooked in a slow cooker for long periods so it's best to add these just before serving.

NOTE FOR VEGANS AND VEGETARIANS
Some of the recipes in the book contain cream, but if you are vegan you can swap this for coconut cream.

CARROT, TOMATO & LENTIL SOUP

This has been a family favourite since my children were little. It is a cheap but very filling and delicious soup. It freezes well, so you can double up the recipe. It is one of those soups that you can usually make with whatever you have in the store-cupboard. This recipe uses tinned tomatoes, but you can use fresh – this is especially good if you have some that need using up.

METHOD

Preheat your slow cooker following the manufacturer's instructions. Add all the ingredients. Season with salt and pepper to taste, and combine well.

Cook on low for 5–6 hours until the vegetables are cooked. When ready to serve, use a stick blender and blend until smooth.

TIP

✳ *Add some heat! If you like soups with a bit of a kick, add a chilli to the recipe and garnish with fresh chopped chillies.*

NUTRITIONAL INFORMATION PER SERVING

212 Kcals

1g fat

34g net carbohydrates

11g protein

INGREDIENTS

1 onion, chopped

400g tin tomatoes
(or 6 chopped fresh tomatoes)

2 tbsp tomato purée

3 carrots, chopped

125g red lentils

1 red pepper (optional),
deseeded and diced

1 tsp paprika

1 tsp dried oregano

500ml hot vegetable or chicken stock

salt and ground black pepper

CHEAT'S MEXICAN POZOLE SOUP

SERVES 4

NUTRITIONAL INFORMATION PER SERVING

288 Kcals

5.1g fat

26g net carbohydrates

30g protein

INGREDIENTS

300g skinless, boneless chicken, diced

400g tin chopped tomatoes

400g tin chickpeas, drained and rinsed

450ml hot chicken stock

1 onion, chopped

2–3 red chillies, to taste, deseeded (unless you like the extra heat) and diced

1 green pepper, deseeded and diced

3 garlic cloves, diced

3 bay leaves

2 tsp ground cumin

2 tsp smoked paprika

2 tsp dried oregano

salt and ground black pepper

chopped avocado and soured cream, to serve

If you like soups with a gentle kick that are also full of flavour, this is one for you to try. Mexican Pozole soup is traditionally made with pork and white hominy, which is a type of corn that you can buy in tins. My version is made with chicken and I have swapped the hominy for chickpeas, but you can use any bean. You can add your own toppings such as creamy avocado or even some soured cream to offset the heat of the chillies. Feel free to adjust the number of chillies to taste.

METHOD

Preheat your slow cooker following the manufacturer's instructions. Add all the ingredients. Season with salt and pepper to taste, and combine well.

Cook on low for 6–7 hours until the chicken is cooked through. When ready to serve, remove the bay leaves and garnish with some chopped avocado and a dollop of soured cream.

CREAMY DHAL SOUP

SERVES 4

This is so easy to make and it costs very little. This version is mild and creamy, but you can make it spicier by adding a few chopped chillies and using a stronger curry powder. Serve with some lovely toasted naan or flatbreads.

METHOD

Preheat your slow cooker following the manufacturer's instructions. Add all the ingredients. Season well with salt and pepper to taste, and combine well.

Cook on low for 6–8 hours.

You can add more stock if needed, depending on the consistency you love.

To serve, garnish with chopped red chillies and serve with naan or flatbreads.

NUTRITIONAL INFORMATION
PER SERVING

437 Kcals

19g fat

43g net carbohydrates

16g protein

INGREDIENTS

1 onion, finely chopped

2 garlic cloves, crushed

3cm piece of fresh ginger, peeled and finely chopped

1 red pepper, deseeded and finely chopped

2 tbsp mild curry powder, or to taste

1 tsp ground turmeric

3 tomatoes, finely chopped

200g red lentils

2 tbsp tomato purée

400g tin coconut milk

500ml hot vegetable stock (or chicken stock), plus extra if needed

salt and ground black pepper

chopped red chillies, to garnish

naan or flatbreads, to serve

SAUSAGE & BEAN SOUP

SERVES 4

NUTRITIONAL INFORMATION PER SERVING

461 Kcals

13g fat

47g net carbohydrates

29g protein

INGREDIENTS

6 sausages

1 onion, finely chopped

2 garlic cloves, crushed

1 celery stick, diced

1 carrot, diced

500g passata

2 tbsp Worcestershire sauce

450ml hot chicken stock

½ tsp dried rosemary

½ tsp dried thyme

2 × 400g tins butter beans, drained and rinsed

salt and ground black pepper

This is a really filling soup, more like a casserole, so be ready for a very hearty meal! It's a great recipe if you have any leftover cooked sausages, as they are always best when cooked before adding them to the slow cooker.

METHOD

Grill, bake or fry the sausages for 15–20 minutes or until cooked through and golden brown. Slice thickly and put to one side.

Preheat your slow cooker following the manufacturer's instructions. Add to your slow cooker the onion, garlic, celery, carrot, passata, Worcestershire sauce and stock. Combine well.

Add the herbs and season with salt and pepper to taste. Cook on low for 5 hours or high for 3 hours.

Add the chopped sausage and butter beans, and continue to cook for 1 hour on high before serving.

CELERY & STILTON SOUP

If you are like me, you might buy a bunch of celery and only use a few sticks, so what do you do with the rest? This is a wonderful soup to use up your celery, and it's also a good way to use any rich cheeses that you might have left over, including Parmesan rinds, as they melt down well. This soup uses Stilton, but any blue cheese, Parmesan or very strong cheese will work well.

METHOD

Preheat your slow cooker following the manufacturer's instructions. Add the onion, celery and potato. Pour over the stock and combine well.

Cook on low for 5 hours or high for 3 hours.

Add the crumbled Stilton and season well with salt and pepper to taste. Continue to cook for 30 minutes. Use a stick blender and blend until smooth. Add the milk if needed to thin the soup. Serve with crusty bread.

NUTRITIONAL INFORMATION PER SERVING

252 Kcals

15g fat

17g net carbohydrates

12g protein

INGREDIENTS

1 small onion, chopped

1 head of celery, chopped

1 potato, roughly chopped

500ml hot vegetable stock

150g Stilton or blue cheese

200ml whole milk or double cream, if needed

salt and ground black pepper

crusty bread, to serve

CREAMY PUMPKIN SOUP

SERVES 4

NUTRITIONAL INFORMATION PER SERVING

219 Kcals

14g fat

18g net carbohydrates

2.9g protein

INGREDIENTS

2 garlic cloves, crushed

1 onion, chopped

1 small pumpkin (about 400g), peeled, deseeded and roughly chopped

1 large carrot, chopped

1 potato, roughly chopped

500ml hot vegetable stock (or chicken or bone stock)

1 tsp ground coriander

1 tsp dried marjoram

150ml double cream (if vegan, use coconut cream), plus 30–50ml extra to serve

salt and ground black pepper

I love pumpkin soup. I usually add lots of spices to my version, but this recipe is designed for all palates to suit the family. It is a mild, creamy soup, ideal for a bonfire night when pumpkins are in abundance, although make sure you use the small pumpkins, as they are more flavoursome than the large ones sold for carving. If you can't get pumpkin, you can use butternut squash instead.

METHOD

Preheat your slow cooker following the manufacturer's instructions. Add the garlic and vegetables. Season with salt and pepper to taste, and combine well. Add the coriander and marjoram and cover with the stock.

Cook on low for 6–7 hours until the vegetables are cooked. Thirty minutes before serving, stir in the double cream. Use a stick blender and blend until smooth. Serve the soup with a dollop of cream in the centre.

TIP

✻ *This recipe can easily be adapted for vegans, just follow the optional suggestions in the list of ingredients.*

CHUNKY CARROT & SWEET POTATO SOUP

SERVES 4

This is a lovely soup, and it's really filling with the added lentils. I have left this chunky with a tasty stock, but you can purée half, or even all, the soup if you prefer a thicker base. If you like things hot, why not add 1 or 2 finely chopped chillies for extra heat?

METHOD

Preheat your slow cooker following the manufacturer's instructions. Make sure that your diced vegetables are all similar sizes suitable for a soup. Add the vegetables, lentils and tomatoes. Cover with the stock and add the herbs and paprika. Season with salt and pepper to taste, and combine well.

Cook on low for 6–7 hours until the vegetables are cooked. Remove the bay leaf and serve the soup with crusty bread.

TIP

✳ *If you want a thicker base to the soup, you can remove 1 or 2 ladlefuls of the soup and purée this before returning the puréed mixture to the remainder of the chunky soup.*

NUTRITIONAL INFORMATION PER SERVING

248 Kcals

1.3g fat

45g net carbohydrates

9.3g protein

INGREDIENTS

1 onion, diced

2 garlic cloves, crushed

2 sweet potatoes, diced

2 carrots, diced

150g dried green lentils (or 400g tin, drained)

400g tin chopped tomatoes

500ml hot vegetable stock (or chicken or bone stock)

1 bay leaf

½ tsp mixed herbs

2 tsp paprika

salt and ground black pepper

crusty bread, to serve

LEEK & POTATO SOUP

SERVES 4

NUTRITIONAL INFORMATION
PER SERVING

295 Kcals

21g fat

22g net carbohydrates

3.7g protein

INGREDIENTS

1 small onion, chopped

1 garlic clove, crushed

1 large potato, roughly chopped

2 leeks, sliced

500ml hot vegetable stock
(or chicken or bone stock)

150ml double cream or full-fat
crème fraîche (vegans can use
coconut cream)

salt and ground black pepper

Leek and potato soup was one of the first soups I ever made, and it is still a family favourite. It is cheap, delicious and very filling – it also freezes well. You can use frozen leeks in this recipe, but make sure they have defrosted before you add them to the slow cooker.

METHOD

Preheat your slow cooker following the manufacturer's instructions. Add the vegetables. Cover with the stock and season with salt and pepper to taste. Combine well.

Cook on low for 6–7 hours until the vegetables are cooked. Thirty minutes before serving, stir in the double cream. Use a stick blender and blend until smooth. Serve with a sprinkling of black pepper on top.

CHUNKY BEAN & VEGETABLE SOUP

SERVES 4

This is a feast of a soup, very filling and packed with nutrients, yet it relies only on store-cupboard and fridge essentials. Serve this with crusty bread or, for a winter-warming treat, some thick, chunky chips. If you are not vegan, it is really delicious when topped with a little grated Parmesan or mature Cheddar cheese.

METHOD

Preheat your slow cooker following the manufacturer's instructions. Add the onion, garlic, celery, red pepper, carrot, tomato purée, tinned tomatoes, beans and stock.

Add the spices and herbs. Season with salt and pepper to taste, and combine well.

Cook on low for 6 hours. Serve with crusty bread or chunky chips.

NUTRITIONAL INFORMATION PER SERVING

217 Kcals

1.6g fat

32g net carbohydrates

11g protein

INGREDIENTS

1 onion, finely chopped

2 garlic cloves, crushed

2 celery sticks, diced

1 red pepper, deseeded and diced

1 large carrot, diced

2 tbsp tomato purée

400g tin chopped tomatoes

2 × 400g tins cannellini beans, drained and rinsed

650ml hot vegetable stock (or chicken stock)

½–1 tsp chilli powder, to taste

½ tsp paprika

1 tsp dried oregano

½ tsp dried thyme

salt and ground black pepper

crusty bread or chunky chips, to serve

CURRIED CREAM OF PARSNIP SOUP

SERVES 4

NUTRITIONAL INFORMATION PER SERVING

441 Kcals

29g fat

34g net carbohydrates

5.2g protein

INGREDIENTS

1 onion, chopped

4 parsnips, unpeeled, cut
into chunks

2 garlic cloves, crushed

3cm piece of fresh ginger,
peeled and crushed

1 large apple, unpeeled, chopped

1 tbsp medium curry powder

550ml hot vegetable stock
(or chicken stock)

200ml double cream or coconut
cream, plus extra cream or milk if
needed, and extra cream to serve

salt and ground black pepper

This is a wonderful, rich, creamy soup, and so cheap to make. This recipe adds a little kick of heat, which I adore, but if you like a milder soup, you can omit the spices. If you are vegan, it works really well with coconut cream. This soup also benefits from a very generous seasoning of black pepper.

METHOD

Preheat your slow cooker following the manufacturer's instructions. Add the vegetables, garlic, ginger and apple, then sprinkle the curry powder over the top.

Pour over the stock, then season well with black pepper and salt to taste if necessary, and stir until combined.

Cook on low for 5 hours. Just before serving, add the cream. Use a stick blender to blend well. Add more cream or milk if needed to achieve the right consistency for your taste. Serve with a swirl of cream.

2

Beef & Venison

Here are some of my family's favourite beef recipes for the slow cooker, which we enjoy regularly. You will also find my delicious Fragrant Beef Rendang Curry on page 198, in the Fakeaway chapter.

BEEF ON A BUDGET

The slow cooker is ideal for cheaper cuts of meat, which tend to be quite tough unless cooked long and slow. I have added some advice on cuts below, but always speak to your butcher to get advice on the best cuts of meat to suit your recipe.

BEST BEEF FOR SLOW COOKING

Most of the recipes in this chapter call for stewing steak, the default terminology, but it is also known as braising steak, which can include skirt, flank or leg – think of the more muscly cuts of meat. Braising steak is also known as chuck or blade steak.

You can also use brisket, which is a tad more fatty but still an excellent choice for slow cooking. It is a little more economical, but don't feel that you have to stick to this; you can switch around and use other cuts, as detailed below.

✻ Beef shin or leg tends to be tough because of how lean and well-used the muscle is, so this benefits from a slow, low cook.

✻ Beef cheeks are very flavoursome as well as being economical.

✻ Oxtail needs a long cook, but it is really bursting with great flavour.

✻ Short ribs are becoming popular and work well when cooked in a similar way to lamb shanks, in a rich sauce, but they have the advantage of being a little cheaper than lamb shanks.

✻ Venison is the meat that comes from deer and is darker in appearance than beef; it has a great flavour and can be used interchangeably with beef in all of the recipes in this chapter. Most venison available in supermarkets is not as gamey as it used to be, as it is not subjected to the traditional maturing process that increases its flavour. The flavour also changes depending on what the animal eats; farmed, corn-fed deer will have a less gamey taste than traditional wild deer. Venison is very nutrient dense, it does not contain as much fat as beef and is high in protein. It is sometimes a little more expensive than beef, but if you see this on offer, it is worth using.

Some people don't like the thought of eating offal; however, these are so nutrient dense and cheap to buy, so do consider using them. You will find a recipe in this chapter with added kidney but also consider liver; both go really well with bacon, venison or lamb dishes.

MINCE

We use a lot of mince in the UK, but it does not always work well for long cooking, so it should be used in the slow cooker for a reduced time. You could speak to your butcher to prepare your mince from a tougher cut of meat, which would work better for longer slow cooking; however, I have included some recipes, such as my Beef Shin Bolognese (page 64), where I use beef shin or cheeks for a long and slow cook and then shred it into flakes once cooked. The result is a little like the way you make pulled pork. When I was growing up, we used to make our mince out of the remains of a cooked joint of beef, using a little hand-held mincer – it's a great idea to save on waste.

BROWNING THE MEAT

All the recipes give the option of sautéing the beef prior to slow cooking. Some people think that this is a waste of time; however, I find that it not only helps to seal the meat but it can also enhance the flavour, plus it stops the meat from bleeding into the stock, which can give a curdled appearance. This is not essential, so you can miss this step if you are someone who prefers to bung it all in the slow cooker at once. I use a multicooker, so I simply switch from sauté to the slow cooker function on my machine, making it much less of a faff. Some regular slow cookers have a sauté option; if your does not, use your hob and transfer the meat to the slow cooker when browned, as given in the recipes – although I appreciate that it is more time-consuming.

HUNGARIAN BEEF GOULASH

SERVES 4

This is an incredibly tasty soup, with a lovely underlying smoky flavour from the paprika that works so well with beef. This recipe includes potatoes, but you can use sweet potatoes if you have these.

METHOD

Preheat your slow cooker following the manufacturer's instructions. Mix the flour and paprika together in a bowl. Dip the beef into the flour mixture until coated, and put it to one side.

If your slow cooker has a sauté option, you can use this: if not, use a frying pan. Heat the oil in the slow cooker or in the frying pan over a medium-high heat. Add the beef, caraway seeds and star anise (if using), the onion and garlic, and cook for 5 minutes, sealing in the meat and flavour. Remove the star anise.

Put in the slow cooker and add the remaining ingredients. Combine well.

Cook on low for 8 hours. Serve with crusty bread.

NUTRITIONAL INFORMATION PER SERVING

371 Kcals

6.9g fat

42g net carbohydrates

31g protein

INGREDIENTS

2 tbsp plain flour

2 tsp paprika

400g stewing beef, diced

1 tsp olive oil or coconut oil

1 tsp caraway seeds (optional)

1 star anise (optional)

1 onion, finely chopped

2 garlic cloves, crushed

1 red pepper, deseeded and diced

2 potatoes, diced

1 carrot, diced

400g tin chopped tomatoes

2 tsp smoked paprika

¼ tsp cayenne pepper

400ml beef stock

salt and ground black pepper

crusty bread, to serve

BEEF SHIN BOLOGNESE

SERVES 4

NUTRITIONAL INFORMATION
PER SERVING

472 Kcals

11g fat

16g net carbohydrates

57g protein

INGREDIENTS

1 onion, finely chopped

2 garlic cloves, crushed

1 red pepper, deseeded and finely diced

1 small carrot, very finely diced

300ml red wine (or beef stock) (*see Tip*)

400g tin chopped tomatoes

1 beef stock cube (or gel)

2 tbsp tomato purée

2 tsp dried oregano

1 tsp paprika

½ tsp dried rosemary

½ tsp dried thyme

600g beef shin or beef cheeks, trimmed and diced (*see* Tip)

salt and ground black pepper

spaghetti and grated Parmesan, to serve

This recipe uses beef shin, which is slow cooked and then shredded prior to serving. You can also use beef cheeks, as both are very flavoursome and pull apart well after a slow cook. This is a lovely variation on the traditional minced beef, as it works so much better on a slow cook than mince (which, if you prefer to use it, only needs 3–4 hours to cook on low heat), with the added bonus of being cheaper.

METHOD

Preheat your slow cooker following the manufacturer's instructions. Add all the ingredients. Season with salt and pepper to taste, and combine well.

Cook on low for 8 hours. When ready to serve, use 2 forks to gently pull the meat apart until it is completely shredded. You might find it easier to remove it from the slow cooker to do this, then return the shredded meat to the slow cooker. Keep on low or warm until you are ready to serve. Serve a generous dollop of the bolognese with spaghetti and top with some Parmesan.

TIPS

✳ *Beef shin has a tough outer sheath that needs to be cut off. Your butcher can do it for you; supermarket meat is usually already trimmed.*

✳ *This recipe uses red wine as a flavouring, but you can omit this if you prefer and add the equivalent amount of beef stock. If you do add red wine, buy the cheapest in the supermarket and keep it just for cooking.*

✳ *Healthy swap: if you are aiming to reduce your carbs, you can swap traditional spaghetti for some spiralised courgette.*

RICH OXTAIL CASSEROLE

SERVES 6

As the name suggests, this is a lusciously rich casserole, bursting with flavour. It is ideal for a dinner party served with parsnip or celeriac mash and steamed green vegetables. Oxtail is an inexpensive cut, but it is really flavoursome. Get your butcher to prepare the oxtail and cut it into pieces for you.

METHOD

Preheat your slow cooker following the manufacturer's instructions. Mix the flour and paprika in a bowl. Dip the oxtail into the flour until lightly coated.

If your slow cooker has a sauté option, you can use this; if not, use a frying pan. Heat the oil in the slow cooker or in the frying pan over a medium heat. Add the beef and bacon, and cook for 5 minutes or until brown, sealing in the meat and flavour.

Put in the slow cooker including any juices, and add the remaining ingredients. Season with salt and pepper to taste, and stir well until combined.

Cook on low for 8 hours or until the oxtail meat easily comes away from the bone.

Remove the bay leaves before serving with parsnip or celeriac mash and steamed green vegetables.

NUTRITIONAL INFORMATION PER SERVING

375 Kcals

16g fat

16g net carbohydrates

27g protein

INGREDIENTS

1 tbsp plain flour

1 tbsp paprika

1kg oxtail, sliced

1 tbsp olive oil

150g cooking bacon or lardons, thickly diced

3 garlic cloves, crushed

2 red onions, chopped

2 carrots, diced

2 celery sticks, diced

1 large parsnip, diced

350ml red wine (or port)

3 tbsp tomato purée

1 beef stock cube (or gel)

2 tsp dried thyme

2 tsp dried parsley

1 tsp dried rosemary

2 bay leaves

salt and ground black pepper

parsnip or celeriac mash and steamed green vegetables, to serve

CREAMY BEEF, SPINACH & BEAN CASSEROLE

SERVES 4–6

NUTRITIONAL INFORMATION PER SERVING

(based on 6 servings)

404 Kcals

11g fat

27g net carbohydrates

39g protein

INGREDIENTS

500g stewing beef, diced

1 large onion, chopped

3 garlic cloves, crushed

½ tsp dried tarragon

½ tsp dried thyme

200ml white wine

200ml beef stock

80g baby leaf spinach (or 4 bales of frozen spinach, defrosted)

2 × 400g tins butter beans (or white kidney beans or cannellini beans), drained and rinsed

2 tbsp full-fat crème fraîche

salt and ground black pepper

A lot of recipes for slow cookers have tomato bases, but this is completely different. It is a light beef casserole in a garlic, wine and creamy sauce. It is really lovely and would also work well if you substitute the beef with chicken.

METHOD

Preheat your slow cooker following the manufacturer's instructions. Add the beef, onion and garlic – there is no need to sauté beforehand.

Add the herbs, wine and stock. Season with salt and pepper to taste, and combine well.

Cook on low for 5–6 hours until the beef is tender. One hour before serving, add the spinach, beans and crème fraîche. Turn to high and continue to cook for the remaining 1 hour until ready to serve.

LOADED COTTAGE PIE

SERVES 4–6

A cottage pie has always been a family favourite for many households, so I had to include a recipe here. This is a very traditional recipe, with a smooth mash topping, but I have filled the meat base with some added vegetables. Mince is better after a low cook for a short time, so in order to cook the vegetables, you need to dice them into small cubes, evenly sized as shown in the photograph.

METHOD

Preheat your slow cooker following the manufacturer's instructions. Add the onion, garlic, celery, pepper, carrot and mince. In a bowl, mix the stock with the Worcestershire sauce and yeast extract and pour this over the mince. Add the marjoram. Season with salt and pepper to taste and combine well.

Cook on low for 5–6 hours until the mixture is cooked through. Twenty minutes before serving, add the mushrooms and peas.

Preheat the oven to 180°C (160°C fan oven) Gas 4. Cook the potatoes in a pan of boiling water for 20 minutes or until soft. Drain in a colander then return to the pan. Mash them with the butter until creamy.

Put the mince in the base of an ovenproof dish. Cover with the mash and finish with some grated cheese. Cook in the oven for 15 minutes or until the mash is golden.

Serve with steamed green vegetables.

TIP

✳ *You can double up the meat base and freeze, ready to make another cottage pie, or make some pastry to use the base for a lovely meat pie.*

NUTRITIONAL INFORMATION PER SERVING

(based on 6 servings)

427 Kcals

20g fat

33g net carbohydrates

25g protein

INGREDIENTS

1 onion, finely chopped

2 garlic cloves, crushed

1 celery stick, finely chopped

1 red pepper, deseeded and finely diced

1 carrot, diced

500g lean minced beef

350ml beef stock

1 tbsp Worcestershire sauce

1 tsp yeast extract, such as Marmite

1 tsp dried marjoram

80g mushrooms, sliced

60g peas, defrosted

800g potatoes, diced

1 tbsp butter

60g mature Cheddar cheese, grated

steamed green vegetables, to serve

CHILLI-INFUSED BEEF STROGANOFF

SERVES 4

NUTRITIONAL INFORMATION PER SERVING

522 Kcals

32g fat

17g net carbohydrates

35g protein

INGREDIENTS

1 tbsp plain flour

2 tsp paprika

500g beef cut into thick strips

1 tsp olive oil

1 onion, finely chopped

2 garlic cloves, crushed

1 red chilli (or to taste), deseeded and finely chopped

1 red pepper, deseeded and finely sliced

150ml white wine

150ml beef or bone stock

300g white mushrooms, sliced

3 tsp Dijon mustard

250ml full-fat crème fraîche or soured cream

1–2 tsp cornflour, if needed

a small handful of fresh parsley, chopped

mashed potato and green steamed vegetables, or chunks of crusty bread, to serve

This is a very simple dish, great for using up tougher cuts of beef such as brisket. I have added some chilli and red peppers and a little spice to help lift it up, but this can be omitted if you prefer a more traditional stroganoff.

METHOD

Preheat your slow cooker following the manufacturer's instructions. First mix the flour and paprika together in a bowl. Dip the beef strips into the flour mixture until coated.

If your slow cooker has a sauté option, you can use this; if not, use a frying pan. Heat the oil in the slow cooker or in the frying pan over a medium-high heat. Add the beef and cook for 5 minutes, sealing in the meat and flavour. Put in the slow cooker and add the remaining ingredients apart from the mushrooms, mustard, crème fraîche, cornflour and parsley, and cook for 5–6 hours on low.

One hour before serving, stir in the sliced mushrooms, Dijon mustard and crème fraîche to form a creamy sauce. If it is too runny, mix the cornflour with 2 tbsp water in a small bowl to form a paste. Stir this into the slow cooker mixture, then turn to high for the remaining 45–60 minutes until it thickens and the mushrooms are cooked. Add the parsley and serve with mashed potato and green steamed vegetables or chunks of crusty bread.

HEARTY BEEF, BEAN & SQUASH CASSEROLE

SERVES 4–6

This is a real winter warmer – and so filling. The recipe uses butternut squash, but you can swap this for pumpkin, sweet potato or even standard potatoes. I have used red kidney beans, but you can use any tinned bean to suit your store-cupboard. Just use up what you have, it will still taste absolutely delicious.

METHOD

Preheat your slow cooker following the manufacturer's instructions. Mix the flour and paprika together in a bowl. Dip the beef in the flour mixture until coated, then put to one side.

If your slow cooker has a sauté option, you can use this; if not, use a frying pan. Heat the oil in the slow cooker or in the frying pan over a medium-high heat. Add the beef, onion and garlic, and cook for 5 minutes, sealing in the meat and flavour.

Put in the slow cooker and add the remaining ingredients apart from the red kidney beans.

Cook on low for 7 hours. Forty-five minutes before serving, add the red kidney beans. (Adding them later prevents them from going mushy or falling apart from a long slow cook.) Serve with crusty bread.

NUTRITIONAL INFORMATION PER SERVING

(based on 6 servings)

290 Kcals

6.9g fat

24g net carbohydrates

30g protein

INGREDIENTS

1 tbsp plain flour

2 tsp paprika

400g stewing beef, diced

1 tsp olive oil or coconut oil

1 onion, finely chopped

2 garlic cloves, crushed

1 red pepper, deseeded and roughly diced

1 red chilli (optional), deseeded and chopped

1 small butternut squash, cubed

1 carrot, diced

400g tin chopped tomatoes

400ml beef stock

1 tsp dried marjoram

½ tsp dried thyme

400g tin red kidney beans, drained and rinsed

crusty bread, to serve

MEATBALLS & SPAGHETTI

SERVES 4

NUTRITIONAL INFORMATION
PER SERVING

405 Kcals

27g fat

7.1g net carbohydrates

32g protein

INGREDIENTS

500g minced beef

1 egg, beaten

40g grated Parmesan (optional)

2 tsp olive oil or coconut oil

spaghetti, to serve

FOR THE SAUCE

400g tin chopped tomatoes

1 onion, finely chopped

3 garlic cloves, crushed

1 chilli (optional), deseeded
and finely chopped

3 tsp dried oregano

1 tsp dried basil

1 tsp dried thyme

salt and ground black pepper

Who doesn't love meatballs with spaghetti? This is my take on
Italian meatballs with a very simple but tasty herby tomato sauce.

METHOD

Preheat your slow cooker following the manufacturer's
instructions. Put all the sauce ingredients in the slow cooker.
Season with salt and pepper to taste, and combine well.

Set to high while you prepare the meatballs.

Put the minced beef in a large bowl. Add the egg and season well
with salt and pepper to taste. Add the Parmesan if using.

Mix the mince with your hands until everything is combined.
Form into 8–12 meatballs, depending on how big you like them.

Heat the oil in a frying pan and fry the meatballs for 5 minutes or
until golden all over to seal them, not to cook them right through.
Sealing helps to prevent them from breaking down when slow
cooked.

Transfer to the slow cooker. Turn the heat down to low and cook
for 2–3 hours. Serve on a bed of spaghetti.

TIP

✳ *If you are a fan of meatballs, why not double the recipe and freeze,
uncooked, the extra meatballs until you are ready to use them? To prevent
the meatballs from sticking together, freeze them on a baking sheet and
bag them once frozen.*

STEAK AND ALE PIE

SERVES 4

Tasty and traditional, steak and ale pie is the perfect dish for a winter's evening. I use shop-bought puff pastry for this, as I love the lightness of the pastry, but you can make your own shortcrust pastry topping if you prefer (it's much cheaper). This recipe also works well with some added kidney (about 200g) or quartered mushrooms (100g). If you don't have any ale, you can use beef stock.

METHOD

Preheat your slow cooker following the manufacturer's instructions. Mix the flour, paprika and mustard powder in a bowl. Dip the meat into the flour mixture until coated.

If your slow cooker has a sauté option, you can use this; if not, use a frying pan. Heat the oil in the slow cooker or in the frying pan over a medium-high heat. Add the meat and cook for 5 minutes, sealing in the meat and flavour. Put in the slow cooker and add the remaining ingredients except the pastry and egg. Season with salt and pepper to taste, and combine well.

Cook on low for 6–7 hours until the steak is tender. One hour before serving, preheat the oven to 180°C (160°C fan oven) Gas 4.

Roll out the puff pastry until 5mm thick. Cut out a pastry lid to fit a deep 28–30cm pie dish. Put the steak mixture into the dish and brush a little water around the edge of the pastry dish to help the pastry to stick. Cut a strip of pastry to go around the edge of the pie dish, and press it onto the rim of the dish. Brush it with water and add the circle of pastry to the top. Using your fingers, pinch the edge to seal and finish the top. Glaze with the beaten egg.

Put the pie into the oven and bake for 30–40 minutes until the pastry is golden and crisp. Serve with steamed green vegetables.

TIP

✳ *Double up and freeze to have your own steak and ale casserole for another day.*

NUTRITIONAL INFORMATION PER SERVING

452 Kcals

19g fat

26g net carbohydrates

37g protein

INGREDIENTS

1 tbsp plain flour

1 tsp paprika

½ tsp mustard powder

500g stewing steak, diced

1 tbsp olive oil

1 onion, chopped

1 tsp dried marjoram

½ tsp dried thyme

400ml ale

1 beef stock cube (or gel)

2 tsp yeast extract, such as Bovril or Marmite

200g puff pastry, defrosted if frozen

1 egg, beaten

salt and ground black pepper

steamed green vegetables, to serve

BEEF LASAGNE

SERVES 4–6

NUTRITIONAL INFORMATION
PER SERVING

(based on 6 servings)

426 Kcals

21g fat

30g net carbohydrates

28g protein

INGREDIENTS

1 tsp olive oil

1 onion, finely chopped

2–3 garlic cloves, to taste,
finely chopped

500g minced beef

400g tin chopped tomatoes

2 tsp tomato purée

1½ tsp Italian or mixed herbs,
plus extra to sprinkle

6–8 no-precook lasagne sheets,
as needed

30g mature Cheddar, grated

salt and ground black pepper

garlic bread and a green salad,
to serve

FOR THE SAUCE

25g butter

30g plain flour or cornflour

500ml whole milk

40g grated Parmesan

You can't really have a family cookbook without lasagne. This recipe can be made with the leftovers to double up as a spaghetti bolognese, or you can follow this easy recipe below. I serve this with garlic bread and a lovely green salad.

METHOD

This recipe needs a little prepping before it goes into the slow cooker. Put the oil in a frying pan over a medium heat. Add the onion, garlic and mince, and cook for 10 minutes or until the bolognese mix has browned. Add the tomatoes, tomato purée and herbs. Season with salt and pepper to taste, and combine well. Leave to one side.

To make the sauce, melt the butter in a small saucepan over a medium heat. Add the flour and stir well with a wooden spoon. Add a little of the milk, stirring continuously to avoid lumps, then gradually add most of the milk. Switch now to a balloon whisk. Continue to stir over a medium heat until the sauce begins to thicken. The balloon whisk will also help to eradicate any lumps that might have materialised. Add more milk as necessary to get the desired thickness. It should be the thickness of custard.

Add the Parmesan and season with black pepper.

Preheat your slow cooker following the manufacturer's instructions. Grease or line the slow cooker with a liner, as this helps to prevent the lasagne from sticking.

Put a layer of bolognese mix in the bottom of the slow cooker, then add a layer of lasagne sheets, followed by a thin layer of sauce. Repeat, finishing with the sauce. Grate some cheese on the top of the sauce, then season and sprinkle with some Italian herbs.

Cook on low for 3–5 hours until the lasagne sheets are cooked. Serve with garlic bread and a green salad.

BEEF STEW & DUMPLINGS

SERVES 6

This is just what you need on a winter's evening. It's a wonderful stew made with very chunky vegetables, mouth-watering beef and topped with fluffy dumplings.

METHOD

Preheat your slow cooker following the manufacturer's instructions. If your slow cooker has a sauté option, you can use this; if not, use a frying pan. Heat the oil in the slow cooker or in the frying pan over a medium-high heat. Add the beef and cooking bacon and cook for 5 minutes or until browned, sealing in the meat and flavour. Put in the slow cooker and add the vegetables, garlic, tomato purée, herbs and stock. Season with salt and pepper to taste, and combine well.

Cook on low for 6–8 hours until the steak is tender.

Meanwhile, make the dumplings. Sift the flour and baking powder into a large bowl, and add the suet, thyme, and salt and pepper. Mix well together, then gradually add a little water, stirring, until you form a firm, thick dough. Add some flour to your hands and form the dough into 6 balls. Leave these to rest until ready to add to the slow cooker.

One hour before serving, remove the lid of the slow cooker, take out the bay leaf and add the dumplings, then turn the heat up to high and cook until the dumplings have puffed up.

TIP

✳ *If you prefer a crisper dumpling, you can bake them in the oven at 180°C (160°C fan oven) Gas 4 for 20 minutes and then add them to the stew just before serving.*

NUTRITIONAL INFORMATION PER SERVING

640 Kcals

28g fat

41g net carbohydrates

54g protein

INGREDIENTS

1 tsp olive oil

750g stewing beef, diced

150g thick cooking bacon, diced

1 large onion, chopped

1 celery stick, chopped

3 carrots, cut into thick chunks

2 potatoes, cut into thick chunks

2 garlic cloves, crushed

1 tbsp tomato purée

2 tsp dried thyme

1 bay leaf

600ml beef stock

salt and ground black pepper

FOR THE DUMPLINGS

125g plain flour, plus extra for dusting

1 tsp baking powder

70g suet

1 tsp thyme

This chapter contains recipes using pork, ham/gammon, sausages and bacon. They all work well in the slow cooker. Pork has the added advantage of being an economical and surprisingly healthy meat, which is high in protein, iron and B vitamins.

Pork is often cheaper than chicken for a meal, especially if you use a cut such as pork loin or chops. You can buy lots of different cuts that work well in the slow cooker. I use pork belly, pork tenderloin, cheek and pork shoulder. Speak to your butcher for cost-cutting suggestions that work well when slow cooked.

SAUSAGES AND BACON

The slow cooker does not brown meat, but sausages do benefit from some colour, so I would advise either cooking them completely by another method and adding them in the last stages of the slow cook, or you could brown them before adding them to the slow cooker. Both methods work well. I strongly advise against using them raw, however, as you will end up not only with a very unappetising sausage, but it will also lose its shape and texture during the longer cooking time.

Bacon can be added to the slow cooker in its raw state and will still give the flavour but it can remain flesh-coloured, so if you want a nice colour as well as a crispy texture to your bacon, you will have to brown/crisp it first.

SIMPLE GAMMON JOINT

SERVES 5–6

I cook a gammon joint most weeks for my family. This is a very simple, basic recipe without any added overpowering flavours, and it's ideal for using the ham for lunches and snacks during the week. Some people like a more flavoursome gammon and cook it in a sweet juice, stock or even cola! I prefer to keep it simple for everyday use and let the natural flavours develop. For a festive flavour, I add cinnamon sticks, cloves and orange zest. Speak to your butcher for budget ham hocks; just like gammon joints, they are economical, tasty and work well in the slow cooker. Cook them in a similar way to cooking a ham or gammon joint.

METHOD

Preheat your slow cooker following the manufacturer's instructions. Spread the onion over the base of the slow cooker. Put the joint onto the onion, then pour over the water or stock. Season with pepper to taste.

Cook on low for 6–8 hours. See tip below for how to make a crisp outer edge for the gammon.

Serve as desired. We like to have ours with a parsley sauce, sautéed potatoes and steamed green veg.

TIP

If you want a crisp outer edge, you can roast the gammon after slow cooking. Follow these simple steps:

✳ *Preheat the oven to 190°C (170°C fan oven) Gas 5. Remove the gammon from the slow cooker and put it in a roasting tray. Score the skin with a sharp knife to form diamonds. If you want to be fancy, you can push some cloves into the tops of each diamond pattern.*

✳ *Roast for 30 minutes until golden. Remove from the oven and allow to rest before slicing.*

NUTRITIONAL INFORMATION PER SERVING

(based on a 1kg joint serving 6 people)

240 Kcals

13g fat

2g net carbohydrates

29g protein

INGREDIENTS

1 onion, sliced

750g gammon joint (any excess fat removed)

750ml water or stock

ground black pepper

parsley sauce, sautéed potatoes and steamed green veg, to serve (optional)

CREAMY MUSTARD PORK

SERVES 4

NUTRITIONAL INFORMATION
PER SERVING

490 Kcals

32g fat

8.8g net carbohydrates

34g protein

INGREDIENTS

600g diced pork loin
(or shoulder)

1 onion, chopped

1 garlic clove, crushed

300ml pork or chicken stock

150ml white wine (or cider,
or more stock)

1 tbsp cornflour

2 tbsp wholegrain mustard

150g full-fat crème fraîche

steamed green vegetables,
to serve

salt and ground black pepper

I use wholegrain mustard a lot with pork as I think they go so well together. This is a flavoursome dish with a delightful creamy sauce with a hint of garlic.

METHOD

Preheat your slow cooker following the manufacturer's instructions. Put the pork, onion, garlic, stock and wine in the slow cooker. Season with salt and pepper to taste, and combine well.

Cook on low for 6 hours. Just before serving, combine the cornflour with a little water in a small bowl to form a paste. Add this to the slow cooker, stirring, then add the wholegrain mustard and the crème fraîche. Stir well.

Turn the heat to high and wait until the sauce has thickened before serving; this should take 5–10 minutes. Serve with steamed green vegetables.

USE-IT-UP SAUSAGE CASSEROLE

SERVES 4–6

This really is a very forgiving casserole, because you can use up any of your vegetables to make it. The only vegetable I would not add is swede, as the flavour can be overpowering. You can also add any bean, and even lentils, to this dish. Here is my version, but feel free to adapt it as your store-cupboard dictates. Quality is everything with sausages, so I always opt for the thick, premium, gluten-free sausages, as they have around 90 per cent meat, without the added nasties. They also hold well in the slow cooker.

METHOD

Preheat your slow cooker following the manufacturer's instructions. If your slow cooker has a sauté option, you can use this; if not, use a frying pan. Heat the oil in the slow cooker or in the frying pan over a medium-high heat, then add the sausages and lardons. Cook for 5 minutes or until the sausages have browned all over. Note: if you prefer, you can fully cook the sausages but do not add these to the slow cooker until the last hour of cooking.

Put in the slow cooker and add the remaining ingredients.

Cook on low for 6 hours. Serve with thick crusty bread and finish with a sprinkle of fresh thyme.

NUTRITIONAL INFORMATION PER SERVING

(based on 6 servings)

352 Kcals

16g fat

26g net carbohydrates

21g protein

INGREDIENTS

1 tsp olive oil or coconut oil

8 pork sausages

125g smoked lardons or cooking bacon, diced

1 large onion, diced

2 garlic cloves, crushed

1 carrot, diced

1 celery stick, diced

2 × 400g tins baked beans

400g tin chopped tomatoes

300ml chicken stock

1 tsp paprika

1 tsp dried thyme

1 tbsp Worcestershire sauce

salt and ground black pepper

a sprinkle of fresh thyme leaves, to garnish

thick crusty bread, to serve

SLOW-COOKED PORK SHOULDER

(based on 8 servings)

159 Kcals

11g fat

2g net carbohydrates

13g protein

INGREDIENTS

2 tbsp olive oil

1.5kg pork shoulder joint,
fat trimmed

4 garlic cloves, roughly chopped

1 large onion, thickly sliced

1 apple, unpeeled and cored

500ml pork or chicken stock

3 or 4 bay leaves, to taste

1 tsp dried thyme

1 tsp dried rosemary

½ tsp peppercorns

Pork shoulder is perfect for roasting as well as slow cooking. This is a very tasty but simple way to cook it. I recommend buying more pork than you need. You can use this recipe for a Sunday roast, then any remaining pork can be shredded, perfect for sandwiches for the week ahead, or to fill tacos, or you could add some jerk sauce to make your own pulled pork.

METHOD

Preheat your slow cooker following the manufacturer's instructions. Heat the oil in a large frying pan over a medium heat, add the pork joint and carefully brown it to add some colour. Remove from the heat.

Put the garlic, onion and apple over the base of the slow cooker. Put the joint on top and pour over the stock. Add the herbs and peppercorns.

Cook on low for 8 hours. Remove from the heat, retaining the juices to make a sauce or gravy. Remember to take out the bay leaves. Slice or shred the pork and serve as you wish.

GARLIC, HERB & MUSTARD PORK TENDERLOIN

SERVES 4

Pork tenderloin is a great option for families. It is incredibly tasty and it is cheap to buy, it absorbs great flavours and is so easy to prepare. This recipe is for a very simple tenderloin with a delicious herb, garlic and mustard crust, but don't be afraid to experiment with other flavours. If you love this recipe, have a little look further in this chapter and you will find a stuffed tenderloin joint; it requires a little more prep, but it is well worth it!

METHOD

Preheat your slow cooker following the manufacturer's instructions. To prepare the tenderloin, remove any skin or fat. Put the onion over the base of the slow cooker. Mix the herbs, garlic, black pepper and mustard together in a small bowl and rub this over the tenderloin.

Put the coated tenderloin on top of the onion slices. Carefully pour the stock into the slow cooker, avoiding the top of the pork, as you don't want to rinse off the mustard coating.

Cook on low for 4–5 hours until the pork is tender. Drain and slice to serve, accompanied with steamed green vegetables and mini roast potatoes.

NUTRITIONAL INFORMATION PER SERVING

237 Kcals

4.6g fat

5.6g net carbohydrates

42g protein

INGREDIENTS

500g pork tenderloin

1 onion, thickly sliced

1 tsp dried parsley

1 tsp dried rosemary

1 tsp dried thyme

3 garlic cloves, crushed

2 tbsp wholegrain mustard

400ml pork or chicken stock

ground black pepper

steamed green vegetables and mini roast potatoes, to serve

TOAD-IN-THE-HOLE

SERVES 4–6

NUTRITIONAL INFORMATION
PER SERVING

(based on 6 servings)

316 Kcals

18g fat

22g net carbohydrates

16g protein

INGREDIENTS

1 tbsp olive oil, plus extra
for greasing

8 good-quality sausages

3 large eggs, beaten

150g plain flour

125ml whole milk

salt and ground black pepper

vegetables and gravy, to serve

I grew up having toad-in-the-hole regularly. I always smile when I think of this recipe, as it has caused quite a bit of confusion in the past for non-UK readers, who wonder what on earth the recipe is going to contain! As stated earlier, I prefer to brown my sausages before placing them in the slow cooker.

METHOD

If your slow cooker has a sauté option, you can use this; if not, use a frying pan. Heat the oil in the slow cooker or in the frying pan over a medium-high heat. Lightly fry the sausages for 5 minutes to give them colour.

Beat the eggs, flour and milk together, then season with salt and pepper to taste.

Thoroughly grease your slow cooker – you can use a slow cooker liner if you prefer.

Put the sausages in the base of the slow cooker. Turn to high, ensuring that the slow cooker is hot before you add the batter. (I have a multi-cooker, so I often keep it on the sauté setting before adding the batter and then I switch it back to the high slow cook setting once the batter has been added.)

Put a tea towel under the lid of the slow cooker, then pop on the lid and push down firmly to ensure that it forms a good seal to help prevent moisture – you don't want soggy batter!

Cook on high for 2–2½ hours until the batter has browned to your liking. If necessary, you can put the slow cooker crock under the grill, if it is ovenproof, to brown the batter for 5 minutes. Serve with vegetables and gravy.

SPICED CHORIZO & CHICKPEA POT

SERVES 4–6

I love the smoky heat of this dish, which is based on the Cuban dish garbanzo fritos. This is packed with spiced chickpeas, smoky chorizo and paprika. It can be made in advance and makes the perfect go-to lunch, either hot or cold.

METHOD

Preheat your slow cooker following the manufacturer's instructions. If your slow cooker has a sauté option, you can use this; if not, use a frying pan. Heat the oil in the slow cooker or in the frying pan over a medium heat. Add the onion, garlic and chorizo, and cook until the sausage starts to release its oils.

Transfer this mixture to the slow cooker and add the remaining ingredients. Season with salt and pepper to taste, and combine everything well.

Cook on low for 5–6 hours. Serve with rice and vegetables or as a side dish.

NUTRITIONAL INFORMATION PER SERVING

(based on 6 servings)

386 Kcals

19g fat

28g net carbohydrates

22g protein

INGREDIENTS

1 tsp olive oil or coconut oil

1 onion, diced

2–3 garlic cloves, to taste, roughly chopped

250g chorizo, sliced

1 chilli, chopped

1 red pepper, deseeded and diced

2 × 400g tins chickpeas, undrained

400g tin chopped tomatoes

1 tbsp Worcestershire sauce

1 tsp ground cumin

2 tsp mild chilli powder

½ tsp chilli flakes
(or 1 tsp chilli powder)

2 tsp smoked paprika

2 tsp dried oregano

rice and vegetables, to serve (optional)

PEAR & MUSHROOM CREAMY PORK

SERVES 4

NUTRITIONAL INFORMATION PER SERVING

529 Kcals

31g fat

20g net carbohydrates

34g protein

INGREDIENTS

600g diced pork loin
(or shoulder)

1 onion, chopped

1 garlic clove, crushed

300ml pork or chicken stock

200ml white wine (or cider,
or more stock)

½ tsp dried tarragon

½ tsp dried sage

½ tsp Dijon mustard

2 pears, unpeeled and cored,
then cut into thick slices
lengthways (or diced if you
prefer smaller chunks)

80g button mushrooms, sliced

3 tsp cornflour

150g full-fat crème fraîche or
double cream

salt and ground black pepper

crusty bread, to serve

We are all used to pork being served with apple, but have you ever thought of pear? This is a great recipe to combine leftover pears with your pork for a really tasty dish. I find the pear is not so overpowering as apple and it allows the flavour of the pork to shine.

METHOD

Preheat your slow cooker following the manufacturer's instructions. Put the pork, onion, garlic, stock, wine, herbs and mustard in the slow cooker. Season with salt and pepper to taste, and combine well.

Cook on low for 6 hours. One hour before serving, add the pears and mushrooms. Combine the cornflour with a little water in a small bowl to form a paste. Stir this into the slow cooker mixture along with the crème fraîche.

Turn to high and cook for 1 hour. Serve with crusty bread.

STUFFED PORK TENDERLOIN

SERVES 4

I love the flavours in this dish: the saltiness of the feta cheese goes so well with spinach and pepper. If you don't have any feta, you could use goat's cheese, or even mozzarella.

METHOD

To prepare the tenderloin, remove any skin or fat. Cut almost in half lengthways: do not cut all the way through, enabling you to open up the tenderloin like a book.

Put on a chopping board and use a meat tenderiser or a rolling pin to bash the tenderloin to help flatten it, as this makes it easier to fill and roll.

Put the feta, peppers and spinach on the tenderloin, leaving a small gap all the way around the edge of the meat. Season with salt and pepper to taste.

Bring the long edges up together and roll. Use wooden cocktail sticks or string to secure the roll all the way along, roughly every 3cm to avoid any gaps.

Preheat your slow cooker following the manufacturer's instructions. Put the onion over the base of the slow cooker.

Mix the herbs, garlic and mustard together in a small bowl and rub or brush this mixture over the tenderloin. Put the coated tenderloin on top of the onion slices.

Carefully pour the stock in the slow cooker, avoiding the top of the pork, as you don't want to rinse off the mustard coating.

Cook on low for 5–6 hours until the pork is cooked through. Drain and slice. Serve with steamed green vegetables and roasted sweet potato.

NUTRITIONAL INFORMATION PER SERVING

386 Kcals

15g fat

9.3g net carbohydrates

51g protein

INGREDIENTS

500g pork tenderloin

200g feta cheese, crumbled

1 red pepper, deseeded and sliced

1 yellow pepper, deseeded and sliced

60g baby leaf spinach

1 onion, thickly sliced

1 tsp dried parsley

1 tsp dried oregano

1 tsp dried thyme

2 garlic cloves, crushed

1 tbsp wholegrain mustard

400ml pork or chicken stock

salt and ground black pepper

steamed green vegetables and roasted sweet potato, to serve

CREAMY PORK CHOPS

SERVES 4

NUTRITIONAL INFORMATION
PER SERVING

444 Kcals

34g fat

8.1g net carbohydrates

27g protein

INGREDIENTS

4 pork chops or loins

1 tbsp olive oil

1 onion, finely chopped

2 garlic cloves, crushed

350ml pork or chicken stock

1 tsp dried thyme

1 tbsp cornflour

150ml full-fat crème fraîche or
double cream

salt and ground black pepper

a small handful of fresh thyme,
to garnish

Pork chops can sometimes be a little dry and uninspiring, but
when we use the slow cooker, they become juicy and succulent.
You can also use pork loin chops for this recipe.

METHOD

If your slow cooker has a sauté option, you can use this; if not,
use a frying pan. Heat the oil in the slow cooker or in the frying
pan over a medium-high heat. Fry the pork chops for 3 minutes
or until they are browned on each side to add colour.

Put the onion over the base of the slow cooker. Add the chops,
garlic, stock, thyme and a generous seasoning of black pepper and
some salt.

Cook on low for 2–3 hours until the chops are cooked through
and tender.

Remove the chops from the slow cooker and put them on a plate
to rest. Turn the slow cooker up to high.

Mix the cornflour with water in a small bowl to form a paste and
stir this into the slow cooker mixture to help thicken it. Add the
crème fraîche.

Return the chops to the slow cooker to heat through again before
serving. Serve with a garnish of fresh thyme.

SAVOURY BACON & CHEESE BREAD PUDDING

SERVES 4–6

This savoury pudding is perfect for a light supper or lunch, or it can even make a very tasty breakfast! There is nothing nicer, in my opinion, than bacon, cheese and onion combined. You can brown this under the grill before serving if you like a nice crispy top, but do remember to use the tea-towel trick (as explained in the method) when baking it in the slow cooker, as this does help to keep the moisture from the top of the savoury pudding.

METHOD

Heat a frying pan over a medium-high heat and cook the bacon until it is browned. Remove from the pan, cut into dice and leave to one side.

Butter the base of your slow cooker, or you can use a liner if you prefer. Mix the milk, eggs and herbs together in a bowl.

Butter the bread and cut each slice into quarters. Put a layer of bread over the base of the slow cooker, then sprinkle it with some of the onion, red pepper, bacon and cheese, ensuring that it is evenly spread. Repeat with the remaining bread and filling to make two or three layers, reserving enough cheese to sprinkle over the top. Pour over the milk mixture. Finish with a sprinkle of cheese. Pop a tea towel under the lid of the slow cooker, then put on the lid and push down firmly to ensure that it forms a good seal to contain any moisture.

Cook on low for 3–4 hours until the bread is soft and soaked with the juices.

You can serve immediately, but if you prefer a very crispy top, put it in an oven preheated to 180°C (160°C fan oven) Gas 4 or under the grill to brown the top until crispy and golden if the crock is ovenproof.

NUTRITIONAL INFORMATION PER SERVING

(based on 6 servings)

341 Kcals

19g fat

21g net carbohydrates

20g protein

INGREDIENTS

6 rashers of thick smoked back bacon

butter, for greasing and buttering

500ml whole milk

3 large eggs

1 tsp dried oregano

1 tsp dried parsley

8 slices of white bread, can be slightly stale

1 onion, diced

1 red pepper, deseeded and diced

100g mature Cheddar cheese, grated

4

Lamb works brilliantly in the slow cooker, benefiting from the long, slow cook. You can buy leg, breast, loin, neck of lamb, shoulder, saddle or rump. As with any meat, speak to your butcher for the best cuts of lamb for your chosen dish.

The term lamb applies only to a young lamb. Lamb is readily available all year around, but it is subtly different depending on the time of year you buy it; spring lamb is a tender meat, but it lacks the flavour of autumn lamb. After the animal has reached around two years of age, it is known as mutton and this has a stronger flavour – almost gamey in taste – which works really well in slow cooking. I have used the name lamb in the recipes, but you can also use mutton. Mutton also works particularly well in curries.

You can get diced lamb suitable for the slow cooker in supermarkets and you can use this for most of the casserole, ragout, curry or tagine dishes in this chapter. If you speak to your butcher, they can be more specific about the cheaper cuts; for example, scrag and middle neck are ideal for slow cooking and are much cheaper cuts. You can also use shoulder, which is cheaper than leg of lamb. Lamb shanks are amazing when cooked in the slow cooker, but they are not the cheapest, which is why I have not included them in this book; however, if you like lamb shanks, you will probably love oxtail or beef short ribs cooked the same way (see Rich Oxtail Casserole on page 67).

LAMB & BUTTERNUT SQUASH TAGINE

SERVES 4–6

Lamb tagines are usually made with apricots and some expensive ingredients, including saffron, but this is my budget version and, to be honest, I prefer it. This reminds me of a wonderful holiday on the Tunisian island Djerba, with the tagine's spicy flavours working well with the sweetness of the squash. I also love the colours – it's a real feast for the eyes. You can swap the squash for sweet potato or even pumpkin, if you like.

METHOD

Preheat your slow cooker following the manufacturer's instructions. If your slow cooker has a sauté option, you can use this; if not, use a frying pan. Heat the oil in the slow cooker or in the frying pan over a medium-high heat. Add the lamb and cook for 5 minutes or until browned, sealing in the meat and flavour.

Put in the slow cooker and add the remaining ingredients apart from the flaked almonds. Season with salt and pepper to taste, and combine well.

Cook on low for 6–8 hours until the lamb is tender. Garnish with coriander leaves and serve with giant couscous and flatbreads.

NUTRITIONAL INFORMATION PER SERVING

(based on 6 servings)

325 Kcals

14g fat

17g net carbohydrates

30g protein

INGREDIENTS

1 tsp olive oil or coconut oil

500g lamb, diced

1 large red onion, chopped

2 chillies, deseeded (unless you like the extra heat) and finely chopped

1 red pepper, deseeded and diced

4cm piece of fresh ginger, peeled and roughly chopped

3 garlic cloves, roughly chopped

1 butternut squash, diced

400g tin chickpeas, drained and rinsed

3–4 tsp ras el hanout, to taste

500ml lamb, bone, chicken or vegetable stock

salt and ground black pepper

fresh coriander leaves, to garnish

giant couscous and flatbreads, to serve

RICH LANCASHIRE HOTPOT

SERVES 6

NUTRITIONAL INFORMATION
PER SERVING

478 Kcals

17g fat

28g net carbohydrates

46g protein

INGREDIENTS

750g diced lamb

2 tbsp plain flour

1 tbsp olive oil or butter

2 lamb's kidneys (about 250g), diced

2 onions, finely chopped

3 carrots, diced

1 parsnip, diced

2–3 potatoes, as required, sliced

2 tsp dried thyme

2 tsp dried rosemary

2 tsp dried mint (or mint sauce)

1 tbsp Worcestershire sauce

450ml lamb, bone, chicken or vegetable stock

100ml red wine (or additional stock)

steamed shredded cabbage, to serve

What can be more traditional for the slow cooker than a lovely Lancashire hotpot? This is my version, which is a little richer and more flavoursome than most. It's a family favourite that is cheap to make and is really satisfying and tasty.

METHOD

Preheat your slow cooker following the manufacturer's instructions. Coat the lamb with flour.

If your slow cooker has a sauté option, you can use this; if not, use a frying pan. Heat the oil in the slow cooker or in the frying pan over a medium-high heat. Add the lamb and cook for 5 minutes until browned, sealing in the meat and flavour. Put in the slow cooker and add the kidneys, onions, carrots and parsnip. Put the sliced potato on the top in an even layer.

Stir the herbs and Worcestershire sauce into the stock and add the wine. Pour this over the vegetables and potato slices.

Cook on low for 7–8 hours until the lamb is tender and the potato is cooked. Sometimes the potatoes can go a bit grey if they are not getting enough liquid. If so, just spoon over some of the liquid or dunk them a little to ensure they get moistened. You can, if you wish, submerge them completely into the hotpot.

Once cooked, if you want to brown the potatoes, you can place the crock, if it is ovenproof, under a preheated grill. Serve with steamed shredded cabbage.

TIP

✳ *If you like, you can sprinkle over some grated cheese before grilling the top.*

SPICED LAMB MEATBALLS WITH COUSCOUS

SERVES 4–6

The flavour of the meatballs in this dish is amazing, especially if you like a Moroccan combination of spices. This is quite a filling dish. It is great with couscous, but you can also eat the meatballs with flatbreads.

METHOD

Preheat your slow cooker following the manufacturer's instructions. Put all the sauce ingredients in the slow cooker. Season with salt and pepper to taste, and combine well. Cook on high for 1 hour. While it cooks, you can get on with preparing the meatballs.

Put the mince in a large bowl. Add the egg and the spices. Season with salt and pepper to taste.

Mix the mince mixture with your hands until everything is combined. Form into 8–12 meatballs, depending on how big you like them.

Heat the oil in a frying pan over a medium-high heat and fry the meatballs for 5 minutes or until they are browned all over. Sealing them helps to prevent them from breaking down during slow cooking. Transfer to the slow cooker.

Cook on high for 1–2 hours until the meatballs are cooked through. Serve on a bed of couscous or with flatbreads.

TIP

* *If you are a fan of meatballs, why not double the recipe and freeze, uncooked, the extra meatballs until you are ready to use them. To prevent the meatballs sticking together, freeze them on a baking sheet and bag them up once frozen.*

NUTRITIONAL INFORMATION PER SERVING

(based on 6 servings)

364 Kcals

21g fat

13g net carbohydrates

29g protein

INGREDIENTS

500g minced lamb

1 egg, beaten

½ tsp cayenne pepper

½ tsp ground cumin

1 chilli, deseeded and chopped (optional)

2 tsp olive oil or coconut oil

salt and ground black pepper

couscous or flatbreads, to serve

FOR THE SAUCE

400g tin chopped tomatoes

150ml lamb, bone, chicken or vegetable stock

1 onion, finely chopped

3cm piece of fresh ginger, peeled and finely chopped

1 green pepper, deseeded and diced

3 garlic cloves, crushed

2 chillies, deseeded (unless you like the extra heat), finely chopped

3 tsp ras el hanout

HEARTY LAMB STEW

SERVES 6

NUTRITIONAL INFORMATION
PER SERVING

483 Kcals

28g fat

22g net carbohydrates

33g protein

INGREDIENTS

1 tbsp olive oil

750g diced lamb

150g thick cooking bacon, diced

2 onions, chopped

3 carrots, cut into thick chunks

2 potatoes, cut into thick chunks

2 garlic cloves, crushed

1 tbsp tomato purée

2 tsp dried thyme

1 bay leaf

2 tsp dried mint (or mint sauce)

750ml lamb, bone, chicken or vegetable stock

mashed potato and green vegetables, to serve

Just what you need on a winter's evening. This is a wonderful stew, made with very chunky vegetables and potatoes. It is always good to keep the vegetables big and chunky, as lamb benefits from a longer cook and that way the vegetables won't fall apart.

METHOD

Preheat your slow cooker following the manufacturer's instructions. If your slow cooker has a sauté option, you can use this; if not, use a frying pan.

Heat the oil in the slow cooker or in the frying pan over a medium-high heat. Add the lamb and cooking bacon and cook for 5 minutes or until browned, sealing in the meat and flavour.

Put in the slow cooker and add the vegetables, garlic, tomato purée, herbs and stock.

Cook on low for 8–10 hours until the lamb is tender. Remove the bay leaf and serve with mashed potato and green vegetables.

GREEK-STYLE LAMB CASSEROLE

SERVES 4

If, like me, you love the flavour of lamb combined with tomato, Mediterranean herbs and aubergine, this dish is for you. It is very tasty, and a meal best served with a green salad – perfect at any time of the year.

METHOD

Preheat your slow cooker following the manufacturer's instructions. Put all the ingredients, apart from the aubergine, in the slow cooker. Season with salt and pepper to taste, and combine well.

Cook on low for 8–10 hours until the lamb is very tender. One hour before serving add the diced aubergine and remove the bay leaf. Serve with a lovely green salad.

NUTRITIONAL INFORMATION PER SERVING

554 Kcals

36g fat

14g net carbohydrates

41g protein

INGREDIENTS

750g diced lamb

2–3 garlic cloves, to taste, chopped

1 red onion, chopped

2 red peppers, deseeded and diced

400g tin chopped tomatoes

2 tbsp sun-dried tomato paste

1 tsp dried thyme

2 tsp dried oregano

½ tsp dried rosemary

1 bay leaf

500ml lamb, bone, chicken or vegetable stock

1 aubergine, diced

salt and ground black pepper

green salad, to serve

BRAISED LAMB CHOPS

SERVES 4

295 Kcals

19g fat

11g net carbohydrates

18g protein

INGREDIENTS

2–3 garlic cloves, to taste,
finely sliced

1 onion, finely chopped

4–8 lamb chops, as required

350ml lamb, bone, chicken or
vegetable stock (or red wine)

1 tbsp wholegrain mustard

2 tsp dried thyme

1 tsp dried rosemary

1 tbsp honey

1 tbsp cornflour

steamed green vegetables,
to serve

Lamb chops are economical to buy. This is a great variation on simple lamb chops where they are braised in a lovely stock flavoured with garlic and thyme, making them moist and succulent.

METHOD

Preheat your slow cooker following the manufacturer's instructions. Put the garlic and onion over the base of your slow cooker. Add the lamb chops.

Mix the stock in a bowl with the mustard, herbs and honey, and pour it over the lamb chops.

Cook on low for 5–6 hours until the lamb chops are tender.

Remove the chops from the stock. Mix the cornflour with a little water in a small bowl and stir this into the stock. Heat on high and stir until thickened. Return the chops to the slow cooker and heat through until ready to serve. Serve with steamed green vegetables.

SHREDDED LAMB

SERVES 6–8

This is a tasty lamb version of pulled pork. The shredded lamb is great with steamed vegetables or you can serve it with a crisp salad. It makes a tasty packed lunch when put in a bread roll with some homemade chutney.

METHOD

Preheat your slow cooker following the manufacturer's instructions. Make incisions into the lamb shoulder using a sharp knife. Put the garlic, chillies, herbs and mustard into a food processor or blender. Add the oil and pulse for 30 seconds.

Rub this mixture over the lamb shoulder, taking care to make sure that it soaks into the slits. If you like a more potent garlic flavour, you can use more garlic (see Tip). Season well with salt and pepper to taste.

Put the slices of onion over the base of the slow cooker. Add the stock, then carefully add the lamb so that it sits on the bed of onions and stock.

Cook on low for 8–10 hours until the lamb is tender and cooked through.

Remove from the slow cooker and carefully shred the meat to use as required.

If you would like a crispy crust, transfer the meat to a roasting pan and put it in an oven preheated to 200°C (180°C fan oven) Gas 6 for 20 minutes or put it under a preheated grill until the outer edge of the garlic coating browns. Serve.

TIP

✳ *If you like a stronger garlic flavour, you can use more garlic cloves: slice them and push them into the incisions.*

NUTRITIONAL INFORMATION PER SERVING

(based on 8 servings)

484 Kcals

32g fat

4.5g net carbohydrates

35g protein

INGREDIENTS

1.5kg lamb leg or shoulder

3 garlic cloves, peeled but left whole (*see also* Tip)

2 chillies, deseeded (unless you like the extra heat)

2 tsp dried rosemary

1 tsp dried thyme

1 tsp dried mint

2 tbsp Dijon mustard

2 tbsp olive oil

2 red onions, sliced

400ml lamb, bone, chicken or vegetable stock

salt and ground black pepper

SLOW-COOKED LEG OF LAMB

SERVES 6–8

NUTRITIONAL INFORMATION
PER SERVING

(based on 8 servings)

494 Kcals

35g fat

3.4g net carbohydrates

33g protein

INGREDIENTS

3–5 garlic cloves, depending on
how garlicky you like it, crushed

2 tsp dried rosemary

juice of 1 lemon

1 tbsp honey

1.5kg leg of lamb

300ml red wine or lamb stock

salt and ground black pepper

This is a deliciously simple dish that makes the most tender lamb.

METHOD

Start preparations the night before. Put the garlic in a small bowl and add the rosemary, lemon and honey. Season with salt and pepper to taste and mix together to form a paste. Rub this into the leg of lamb. Cover and put in the fridge overnight.

Preheat the slow cooker, following the manufacturer's instructions. Put the lamb in the slow cooker and pour the wine around the sides of the lamb.

Cook on low for 8 hours. If you would like a crispy crust, transfer the meat to a roasting pan and put it in an oven preheated to 200°C (180°C fan oven) Gas 6 for 20 minutes or put it under a preheated grill until the outer edge of the lamb and garlic coating browns.

5

Chicken

Versatile chicken is one of the most popular meats in the UK. It works well in the slow cooker but it does not need the really long, slow cook required by tougher cuts of meat, such as lamb or beef. If you are a fan of chicken, don't forget to also look at the Fakeaways chapter on page 177, as there are several other chicken recipes there, including Chicken Biryani, Chicken Tikka Masala and Chicken Chow Mein.

Most families opt for chicken breast, but I would recommend using thighs and leg meat, as these are much more suited to longer cooks, producing a better flavour than breast, and they have the added bonus that they are often much cheaper to buy. You can buy them skinless and boneless so that they are suitable for all the family to enjoy.

If you are roasting a chicken for Sunday lunch, buy a size bigger than you usually would and use the leftover meat (from all over the chicken, not just the breast and legs), to make yourself a chicken pie, a chicken crumble, chicken fajitas or enchiladas – or even a curry. Don't forget to save the bones. The carcass makes an excellent and very nourishing chicken stock (see page 35 for my stock recipe).

POACHED CHICKEN

If you are fed up with dry chicken that has been cooked in the oven, you can use your slow cooker to poach it. This is great if you want lovely tender chicken for salads or sandwiches. Simply add your chicken breast or thighs to the slow cooker, cover with chicken stock and cook on low for 4–5 hours (or high for 2–3 hours) until tender. Remove the chicken from the stock, but retain the stock, which can be put in the fridge or frozen to use for another dish.

MEDITERRANEAN CHICKEN WITH BLACK OLIVES

SERVES 4

This is a richly flavoured chicken dish with thick peppers and black olives in a tomato and garlic sauce – so simple yet so tasty! I make mine with chicken thighs with the skins on, as these are less than half the price of skinless; however, if you prefer them without skin, you can use those. This recipe does benefit from the chicken being browned before adding it to the slow cooker, especially if you are using, as I do, chicken thighs with the skins on.

METHOD

Preheat your slow cooker following the manufacturer's instructions. If your slow cooker has a sauté option, you can use this; if not, use a frying pan. Heat the oil in the slow cooker or in the frying pan over a medium-high heat and fry the chicken for 5 minutes or until the skin is a nice golden brown. Transfer to the slow cooker.

Add the remaining ingredients, leaving the whole olives for a garnish.

Cook on low for 6–8 hours until the chicken is tender. Serve sprinkled with the remaining olives.

NUTRITIONAL INFORMATION PER SERVING

225 Kcals

12g fat

7g net carbohydrates

22g protein

INGREDIENTS

1 tsp olive oil

400g chicken thighs (with or without skin)

3 red peppers, deseeded and thickly sliced

3 garlic cloves, finely chopped

1 onion, finely chopped

400g tin chopped tomatoes

250ml chicken stock

½ tsp dried rosemary

¼ tsp dried basil

½ tsp dried thyme

1 tsp dried oregano

50g pitted black olives, half cut in half, half left whole for garnish

salt and ground black pepper

CHICKEN, LEEK & SPINACH CRUMBLE

SERVES 4–6

NUTRITIONAL INFORMATION PER SERVING

(based on 6 servings)

438 Kcals

25g fat

26g net carbohydrates

26g protein

INGREDIENTS

1 tsp olive oil or a knob of butter

500g boneless chicken thighs, diced

1 leek, finely chopped (or onion)

1 garlic clove, crushed

½ tsp dried tarragon

1 tsp dried thyme

300ml chicken stock

180g full-fat cream cheese

75g peas, defrosted

75g spinach (or frozen, defrosted)

1 tbsp cornflour (if needed)

salt and ground black pepper

steamed green vegetables,
to serve

FOR THE CRUMBLE TOPPING

150g fresh breadcrumbs
(or use stale bread)

50g oats

40g Parmesan or mature
Cheddar cheese, grated

50g butter, cut into small pieces

We think of a crumble as a sweet dish, but it works brilliantly as a savoury dish too. This crumble uses breadcrumbs, which could come from leftover stale bread or even the crusts. You can use lots of things to make a crumble top: pork scratchings, cheese, Parmesan, leftover savoury biscuits – use your imagination and use up what you have in the kitchen. The crumble topping is added after the slow cook, and benefits from a quick blast under the grill to brown before serving.

METHOD

Preheat your slow cooker following the manufacturer's instructions. If your slow cooker has a sauté option, you can use this; if not, use a frying pan. Heat the oil in the slow cooker or in the frying pan over a medium heat. Add the chicken and leek, and cook for 5 minutes until the leek starts to soften and the chicken seals. (If you prefer, you can skip this step. This can result in the chicken flaking into the sauce a little, but it will not affect the taste at all.)

Put the chicken and leek in the slow cooker. Add the garlic, herbs, stock and cream cheese. Season with salt and pepper to taste, and combine well.

Cook on low for 5–6 hours until the chicken is tender.

Turn up to high and stir in the peas and spinach. If the sauce is too thin for your liking, mix the cornflour with a little water in a small bowl and stir it into the sauce. Cook for 10 minutes.

Meanwhile, to prepare your crumble topping, put the breadcrumbs, oats and cheese in a bowl. Use your fingertips to rub in the butter. Season with salt and pepper to taste.

Transfer the chicken mixture from the slow cooker to a warm ovenproof serving dish. Add the crumble topping and spread until covered evenly. Pop under a preheated grill for 5 minutes or until golden and bubbling. Serve immediately with some steamed green vegetables.

BRUNSWICK-STYLE STEW

This is a delicious stew of chicken, vegetables and beans in a fragrant tomato sauce. It is very filling and perfect for the slow cooker. You can use cooked, leftover chicken in this, but if you do, add this only in the last hour of slow cooking or it will fall apart. You can also swap the chicken for turkey, pork or even beef, if you prefer.

METHOD

Preheat your slow cooker following the manufacturer's instructions. Add all the ingredients apart from the sweetcorn and beans. Season with salt and pepper to taste, and combine well.

Cook on low for 5–6 hours until the chicken is tender. One hour before serving, you can use a fork and start to very gently shred some of the chicken, leaving some shredded and some in large pieces.

Add the sweetcorn and beans, and combine well. Cook for the remaining 1 hour. Remember to remove the bay leaf. Serve with crusty bread.

NUTRITIONAL INFORMATION PER SERVING

305 Kcals

12g fat

17g net carbohydrates

28g protein

INGREDIENTS

100g smoked cooking bacon, diced (or lardons or pancetta)

500g boneless, skinless chicken pieces, diced

1 carrot, diced

1 celery stick, diced

1 red pepper, deseeded and diced

400g tin chopped tomatoes

1 tbsp tomato purée

½ tsp dried thyme

1 bay leaf

400ml chicken stock

100g tinned or frozen and defrosted sweetcorn

400g tin cannellini or white kidney beans, drained and rinsed

salt and ground black pepper

crusty bread, to serve

RUSTIC CHICKEN CASSEROLE

SERVES 4–6

NUTRITIONAL INFORMATION
PER SERVING

(based on 6 servings)

429 Kcals

17g fat

23g net carbohydrates

41g protein

INGREDIENTS

1 large onion, finely chopped

2 garlic cloves, crushed

1 celery stick, chopped

2 carrots, diced

400g tin tomatoes

500g skinless chicken pieces
(thighs or breast)

100g lardons or cooking bacon,
diced (optional)

400g tin mixed beans, drained
and rinsed

400ml chicken stock

1 tsp chicken seasoning

1 tbsp Worcestershire sauce

1 tsp dried thyme

1 bay leaf

1 small handful of fresh
chopped parsley

salt and ground black pepper

steamed vegetables and mashed
potato, to serve

This is a great recipe to use up any of your leftovers while
providing a delicious and wholesome casserole, perfect to fill your
family with goodness.

METHOD

Preheat your slow cooker following the manufacturer's
instructions. Add all ingredients,, apart from the beans.

Cook on low for 6–8 hours, or if you want a faster meal, turn to
high for 4–5 hours until the chicken is tender. One hour before
serving, add the beans, remove the bay leaf and cook for the
remaining hour. Serve with steamed vegetables and mashed potato.

CHICKEN & MUSHROOM PIE

SERVES 6

I love a nice chicken pie, and this one is absolutely delicious. Sometimes I add some diced ham hock if I have any that needs using up. I use shop-bought puff pastry for this one, as I love the lightness of the pastry, but you can make your own shortcrust pastry topping if you prefer (it will be much cheaper).

METHOD

Preheat your slow cooker following the manufacturer's instructions. Put the chicken, onion, stock and thyme into your slow cooker. Cook on high for 1–1½ hours until the chicken is tender.

Preheat the oven to 180°C (160°C fan oven) Gas 4. Add the cream cheese and mushrooms to the chicken mixture. Season with salt and pepper to taste, and combine well. If the stock needs thickening, mix the cornflour with a little cold water in a small bowl and stir into the stock until it thickens.

Roll out the puff pastry on a lightly floured work surface to approximately 5mm thickness. Cut out lids, or a lid, to fit individual pie dishes or one large pie dish.

Put the chicken mixture into the pie dishes and brush a little water around the edges to help the pastry to stick. Cut a strip of pastry to go around the edges of the pie dish, and press it onto the rim. Brush it with water and add the lid to the top. Pinch the edge to seal and finish the top. Glaze with the egg.

Put the pies into the oven and bake for 25–35 minutes until the pastry is golden and crisp. Serve with steamed green vegetables.

TIP

✳ *To make your own shortcrust pastry, use 300g of flour and add 150g cold butter, cut into small pieces. Rub the butter into the flour using your fingertips until it resembles breadcrumbs. Stir in just enough cold water to form a dough. Rest in the fridge for 10 minutes before rolling.*

NUTRITIONAL INFORMATION PER SERVING

471 Kcals

27g fat

29g net carbohydrates

27g protein

INGREDIENTS

500g skinless, boneless chicken thighs, diced

1 large onion, chopped

350ml chicken stock

½ tsp dried thyme

200g full-fat cream cheese

200g button mushrooms. sliced

1–2 tsp cornflour, if needed

325g puff pastry, defrosted if frozen

flour, for dusting

1 egg, beaten

salt and ground black pepper

steamed green vegetables, to serve

PULLED CHICKEN CASSEROLE

SERVES 4

NUTRITIONAL INFORMATION PER SERVING

411 Kcals

12g fat

31g net carbohydrates

37g protein

INGREDIENTS

1 onion, chopped

1 red or orange pepper, deseeded and thickly diced

2 garlic cloves, crushed

1–2 chillies, to taste, deseeded (unless you like the extra heat), chopped, plus extra to garnish

1 tsp chilli powder

2 tsp Italian herbs (or mixed herbs or oregano)

400g tin chopped tomatoes

2 tbsp tomato purée

300ml chicken stock

500g boneless, skinless chicken thighs or breast

200g tin sweetcorn, drained (or frozen, defrosted)

400g tin cannellini beans, drained and rinsed

salt and ground black pepper

crusty bread, to serve

This wonderful casserole is a real family favourite. It uses everyday ingredients that you will find in your store-cupboard and fridge. It's so easy, so tasty and so filling.

METHOD

Preheat your slow cooker following the manufacturer's instructions. Put all the ingredients in the slow cooker apart from the sweetcorn and beans. Season with salt and pepper to taste, and combine well.

Cook on low for 6–8 hours until the chicken is tender. Thirty minutes before serving, use 2 forks to gently shred the chicken.

Add the sweetcorn and beans. Cook on high for 30 minutes, then serve with crusty bread.

CHAKHOKHBILI

SERVES 4

This is my nod to a Georgian tomato and pepper chicken stew.
It is one of those meals where you just want to get chunks of thick
bread and dip them into the rich tomato sauce. I use thighs for this
recipe, but you can use breast if you prefer, with or without skin.
I would advise that you sauté them first, as shown in the recipe,
as this adds colour to the chicken.

METHOD

Preheat your slow cooker following the manufacturer's
instructions. If your slow cooker has a sauté option, you can use
this; if not, use a frying pan. Heat the oil in the slow cooker or in
the frying pan over a medium-high heat. Add the chicken and fry
it for 5 minutes to brown it.

Put the chicken and all the remaining ingredients in the slow
cooker. Season with salt and pepper to taste, and combine well.

Cook on low for 6–8 hours until the chicken is tender. Remove the
bay leaves, garnish with fresh coriander and serve with some thick
crusty bread.

NUTRITIONAL INFORMATION
PER SERVING

335 Kcals

13g fat

19g net carbohydrates

32g protein

INGREDIENTS

2 tbsp olive oil

600g chicken thighs or breast,
with or without skin

1 large onion, diced

2 garlic cloves, crushed

2 red peppers, deseeded and
sliced

2 × 400g tins chopped tomatoes

200ml chicken stock

1 tsp paprika

1 tsp dried parsley

2 tsp freeze-dried coriander

2 bay leaves

2 tsp honey (or sugar)

salt and ground black pepper

chopped fresh coriander,
to garnish

thick crusty bread, to serve

CHICKEN MEATBALLS IN CREAMY MUSHROOM & THYME SAUCE

SERVES 4

NUTRITIONAL INFORMATION
PER SERVING

524 Kcals

19g fat

19g net carbohydrates

68g protein

INGREDIENTS

500g minced chicken or turkey

1 garlic clove, crushed

1 tsp onion powder

75g fresh breadcrumbs
(or use stale bread)

1 egg, beaten

olive oil, for greasing or frying

salt and ground black pepper

steamed green vegetables,
to serve

FOR THE SAUCE

1 onion, finely chopped

2 garlic cloves, crushed

300ml chicken stock

80g mushrooms, sliced

1 tsp dried thyme

200g full-fat cream cheese

These meatballs can be made in advance and the sauce takes an hour on high, so this is one of those rare slow cooker recipes, that, with planning, you can cook quickly. The chicken meatballs also freeze well, so why not double up the recipe and freeze some? Remember to add the meatballs to the slow cooker only when they are defrosted. Once you try this recipe, it will become a family favourite!

METHOD

Preheat your slow cooker following the manufacturer's instructions. To make the sauce, put the onion, garlic, chicken stock, mushrooms and thyme in the slow cooker. Season with salt and pepper to taste, and combine well.

Cook on high for 1 hour.

Meanwhile, prepare the meatballs. Preheat the oven to 200°C (180°C fan oven) Gas 6 and grease a baking tray if you want to oven-cook them (or you can fry them if you prefer). Put the minced chicken and the remaining ingredients, except the oil, in a bowl and season with salt and pepper to taste. Mix well together, then form into 8–12 meatballs, depending on how big you like them. I like mine quite chunky.

Put the meatballs on the prepared baking tray and cook in the oven for 20 minutes or until golden. (Alternatively, fry them in a frying pan with some olive oil for 10 minutes until golden and crispy.)

Add the cream cheese to the mixture in the slow cooker and combine well until it is dissolved into the stock, then add the cooked meatballs. Continue to cook on high for another 30–45 minutes until everything is thoroughly heated through. Serve with steamed green vegetables.

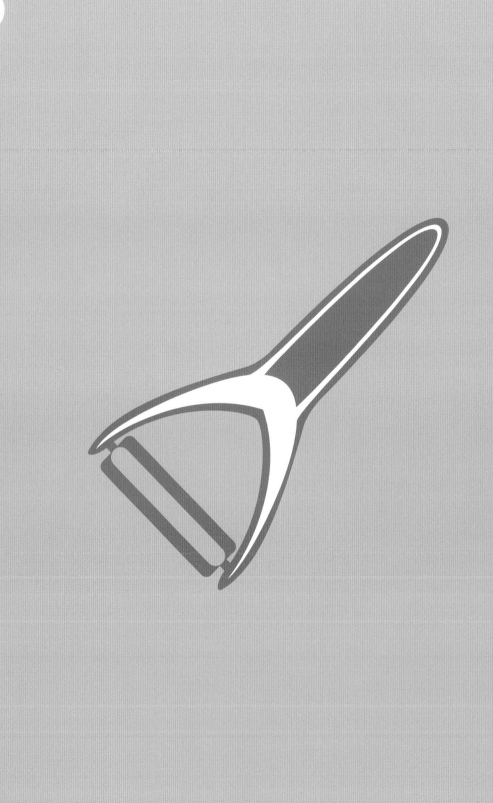

6

Although this chapter is suitable for vegans and vegetarians, don't pass it by because you think that the recipes are not interesting if you eat meat. These recipes are all delicious and suitable for meat eaters as well as vegetarians. They are family favourites packed with flavour.

Vegan and plant-based lifestyles are growing increasingly popular. Some people have adopted this way of eating 100 per cent of the time, whereas others try to have one or two days a week when they are vegan or vegetarian. I would encourage everyone who is thinking about vegan and veganism to opt for a real-food diet and to avoid the 'fake' manufactured products that are highly processed and highly inflammatory due to the high levels of seed oils and unnatural ingredients used in them. It is so important to ensure that you have enough quality nutrients in your diet, in particular good protein from a variety of foods, healthy fats, minerals and vitamins. You will find it harder to get a complete protein profile, good-quality omega 3, iron and vitamin B12 from a completely vegan diet, making it even more vital to get your food from good natural sources that are nutrient rich. (For more information, you could check out my book *The Part-Time Vegan*.)

PROTEINS

There are curds that you can use as a vegetarian protein source, such as paneer (which is a curd made from cow's milk), or the vegan forms made from soya: tofu or tempeh. You can also include beans and pulses, which are cheap but nutritious and help to bulk out meals. Nuts and seeds, including nut butter, are also very healthy options.

The slow cooker works well with both vegan and vegetarian dishes. Here is a selection of my personal favourites.

MEDITERRANEAN STUFFED PEPPERS

SERVES 4

Stuffed peppers can be prepared in advance. They are a great dish for using up the peppers that you might have left in your salad drawer, as you only use half a pepper per serving for this dish. I have used very economical couscous with tomato as a base, dressed with some salty feta cheese to offset the sweetness of the peppers.

METHOD

Preheat your slow cooker following the manufacturer's instructions. Put the couscous in a bowl and add the hot water, then leave to rest for 5 minutes.

Meanwhile, finely chop half the black olives, leaving the remaining half to one side for serving.

Put the onion into the bowl with the couscous and add the sun-dried tomatoes, half the feta, the chopped olives, oregano, basil and mint. Season with salt and pepper to taste, and combine well.

Spoon this mixture into your peppers, leaving the remaining feta and halved olives to one side.

Put the peppers in your slow cooker and drizzle with the olive oil.

Cook on low for 5–6 hours until the peppers are cooked through and tender.

When ready to serve, add the remaining feta and olives. Garnish with some basil leaves. Serve with a lovely salad and sweet potato wedges.

NUTRITIONAL INFORMATION PER SERVING

398 Kcals

24g fat

31g net carbohydrates

11g protein

INGREDIENTS

150g couscous

300ml boiling water

50g pitted black olives, halved

1 small onion, very finely chopped

75g (about 12) sun-dried tomato pieces, drained and halved

125g feta cheese, finely chopped

1 tsp dried oregano

½ tsp dried basil

1 tsp dried mint

2 peppers, halved lengthways and deseeded

2 tbsp olive oil

fresh basil leaves, to garnish

salad and sweet potato wedges, to serve

BEAN & SPINACH POT

SERVES 4

NUTRITIONAL INFORMATION PER SERVING

321 Kcals

2.2g fat

47g net carbohydrates

18g protein

INGREDIENTS

2 × 400g tins white kidney beans or butter beans, drained and rinsed

400g tin chopped tomatoes

2 garlic cloves, finely chopped

1 onion, finely sliced

2 red peppers, deseeded and finely sliced

350ml vegetable stock

1 tsp paprika

2 tbsp tomato purée

1 tsp dried oregano

½ tsp dried thyme

80g baby leaf spinach (or frozen spinach, defrosted)

a small handful of fresh basil leaves (optional)

salt and ground black pepper

crusty bread, to serve

This dish is heavenly with some thick toasted bread and, for extra decadence, if you are not vegan, add a sprinkle of salty feta cheese. You can use white kidney beans (normally found in the world foods aisle in your supermarket), butter beans or cannellini beans in this dish.

METHOD

Preheat your slow cooker following the manufacturer's instructions. Put all the ingredients, apart from the spinach and basil leaves, in the slow cooker. Season with salt and pepper to taste, and combine well.

Cook on low for 6–8 hours until rich and tender.

Thirty minutes before serving, add the spinach and the basil leaves. Stir well.

Cook on high with the lid off for 30 minutes. Serve with some crusty bread.

JACKFRUIT PULLED 'PORK'

SERVES 6

If you have not heard of jackfruit, it is the new wonder fruit that is transforming vegan food. Jackfruit is a very large fruit. When ripe it is very tropical in taste but the jackfruit used in cooking is green, unripe and does not really have much of a taste, so it is great to absorb other flavours. It is also very fibrous, so when cooked and 'pulled' apart it has the same look and texture as pulled pork, although unlike pork, it is very low in protein. You can buy jackfruit in the UK in tins ready to use.

METHOD

Preheat your slow cooker following the manufacturer's instructions. Put all the ingredients in the slow cooker. Season with salt and pepper to taste, and combine well.

Cook on low for 4 hours. Use a fork to pull the jackfruit apart to create a pulled-pork effect. Continue to do this until all the jackfruit pieces are shredded.

Cook on low for another 20–30 minutes until thoroughly heated through before serving. Serve in a toasted bun with coleslaw or slices of avocado, lettuce and tomato.

NUTRITIONAL INFORMATION PER SERVING

186 Kcals

0.7g fat

41g net carbohydrates

2.2g protein

INGREDIENTS

2 × 400g tins jackfruit in water, drained

1 red onion, finely chopped

2 garlic cloves, crushed

1–2 chillies, to taste, deseeded (unless you like the extra heat), finely chopped

1 tbsp apple cider vinegar

3 tsp smoked paprika

2 tsp dried oregano

2 tsp Tabasco sauce

1 tsp ground cumin

1 tsp ground cinnamon

400g tin chopped tomatoes

4 tbsp barbecue sauce

100ml vegetable stock

salt and ground black pepper

toasted bun with coleslaw or slices of avocado, lettuce and tomato, to serve

ITALIAN STUFFED PEPPERS

SERVES 4

These are so tasty and can be prepared in advance, ready to pop in the slow cooker when needed. I have used mozzarella cheese, but if you are vegan, you could use a vegan cheese, or simply leave this out – it will still be very tasty!

NUTRITIONAL INFORMATION
PER SERVING

359 Kcals

19g fat

31g net carbohydrates

12g protein

INGREDIENTS

60g brown basmati rice (or use 250g cooked brown basmati rice)

1–2 tbsp olive oil, for greasing

4 peppers (any colour)

1 onion, finely chopped

2 garlic cloves

1 courgette, diced

2 tbsp sun-dried tomato paste

400g tin chopped tomatoes

50g black or green olives (optional)

2 tsp Italian mixed herbs

150g mozzarella, sliced or grated

salt and ground black pepper

green salad with a drizzle of balsamic vinegar, to serve

METHOD

If using raw rice, rinse the basmati rice under cold water and cook in a pan of boiling water for 20 minutes or until tender. Drain in a sieve.

Oil the lining of the slow cooker well to ensure that the peppers don't stick. Preheat your slow cooker following the manufacturer's instructions.

Cut the tops off the peppers but keep them to one side. Scoop out the insides of the peppers ready to fill them.

Put the rice and all the remaining ingredients apart from the cheese in a bowl. Season with salt and pepper to taste, and combine well. Spoon this mixture into the peppers.

Top with the cheese and pop on the pepper lids.

Put in the slow cooker. Put a tea towel over the top of the slow cooker, then pop on the lid and push down firmly to ensure that it forms a good seal.

Cook on high for 2–3 hours until cooked through and tender. (If your cooker is old and food tends to catch in places, it is better to turn it to low and cook it for longer to avoid any burning edges.) Serve with a green salad with a drizzle of balsamic vinegar.

EASY MACARONI CHEESE

SERVES 4

This really is stupidly easy, just add all the ingredients to the pot and walk away. It is pure comfort food, so get your favourite book ready, as you will soon be curling up somewhere with a satisfying bowl of mac 'n' cheese.

METHOD

Preheat your slow cooker following the manufacturer's instructions. Add all the ingredients to the slow cooker. Season with salt and pepper to taste, and combine well.

Cook on low for 2 hours or until the pasta is cooked. Serve immediately.

NUTRITIONAL INFORMATION PER SERVING

463 Kcals

25g fat

33g net carbohydrates

25g protein

INGREDIENTS

1 litre whole milk

250g mature Cheddar cheese, grated

150g full-fat cream cheese

40g vegetarian Parmesan cheese

1–2 tbsp nutritional yeast flakes, to taste (optional)

½ tsp English mustard powder (optional)

400g dried macaroni or pasta

salt and ground black pepper

'THROW IT IN' VEGAN BEAN STEW

SERVES 4

NUTRITIONAL INFORMATION
PER SERVING

345 Kcals

2.1g fat

51g net carbohydrates

20g protein

INGREDIENTS

1 onion, finely chopped

2 garlic cloves, crushed

1 large red pepper, deseeded
and diced

1 celery stick, chopped (optional)

2 carrots, chopped into bean-
sized chunks

400g tin chopped tomatoes

2 tbsp tomato purée

300ml vegetable stock

1 tsp dried mixed herbs

2 × 400g tins mixed beans,
drained

75g frozen peas, defrosted

salt and ground black pepper

boiled white rice, to serve

This really does say it all. It is a perfect store-cupboard, throw-it-in bean stew – tasty, filling, nutrient dense and cheap to make. You can also double up this recipe and use this base for a vegan crumble – just add some savoury crumble toppings. Rub some vegan butter into your dry crumble mix in a ratio of one part butter to two parts crumble mix. I use a blend of flour, oats and seeds.

METHOD

Preheat your slow cooker following the manufacturer's instructions. Add all the ingredients, apart from the beans and frozen peas. Season with salt and pepper to taste, and combine well.

Cook on low for 5–6 hours until the vegetables are softened and the sauce is rich.

Add the beans and peas and cook on high for a further 30–45 minutes. Serve with fluffy white rice.

TIP

✳ *There is very little fat in this recipe, so why not add some healthy fat by topping this stew with some fresh, chopped avocado?*

BROCCOLI, SPINACH, CHEESE & WALNUT CRUSTLESS PIE

CUTS INTO 6–8 SLICES

This is an easy recipe for the slow cooker, and one of my favourites. I love this when it's loaded with cheese – you can use up any leftover vegetarian Parmesan for a more intense cheese flavour.

METHOD

Preheat your slow cooker following the manufacturer's instructions. Grease the slow cooker very well. (Alternatively, you can use a cake liner or line the slow cooker with baking parchment, which does make it easier to remove the quiche.)

Put the broccoli evenly over the base of your slow cooker. Add the spinach and walnuts, and top with the onion and cheese.

Beat the eggs and milk together in a jug until well combined. Add the herbs and season well with salt and pepper. Pour into the slow cooker, ensuring that everything is covered.

Cook on high for 1–2 hours or low for 3–4 hours or until firm to the touch. Serve hot or cold.

NUTRITIONAL INFORMATION PER SERVING

(based on 8 slices)

228 Kcals

17g fat

4.5g net carbohydrates

14g protein

INGREDIENTS

olive oil, for greasing

½ head of broccoli, cut into small florets

80g baby leaf spinach (or frozen spinach, defrosted)

60g walnuts, roughly chopped

1 small onion, finely chopped

150g mature Cheddar cheese (or any strong cheese), grated

6 eggs, beaten

300ml whole milk or double cream

1 tsp dried oregano

1 tsp dried parsley

salt and ground black pepper

BEAN & VEGETABLE CRUMBLE

SERVES 6

NUTRITIONAL INFORMATION PER SERVING

335 Kcals

15g fat

36g net carbohydrates

8.8g protein

INGREDIENTS

1 red onion, sliced

2 garlic cloves, crushed

1 red pepper, deseeded and thickly diced

1 courgette, thickly diced

2 celery sticks, diced

1 carrot, diced

1 aubergine, thickly diced

400g tin chopped tomatoes

2 tbsp tomato purée

2 × 400g tins mixed beans, drained and rinsed

2 tsp paprika

2 tsp Italian mixed herbs (or dried oregano)

a handful of fresh chopped parsley

400ml vegetable stock

3 heaped tsp cornflour, if needed

salt and ground black pepper

steamed green vegetables, to serve

This recipe is made in two parts: first you cook the vegetables and beans, then you add the crumble mixture. It is a lovely filling recipe, ideal for winter evenings.

METHOD

Preheat your slow cooker following the manufacturer's instructions. Put the red onion and garlic and the other ingredients, apart from the cornflour and crumble topping, in the slow cooker. Season with salt and pepper to taste, and combine well.

Cook on low for 4 hours, or set to high and cook for 2 hours.

Meanwhile, make the topping. Put the flour and butter in a large bowl and rub the butter into the flour using your fingertips until it looks like fine breadcrumbs. Stir in the oats and seeds.

Remove the lid of the slow cooker and stir the vegetable and bean mixture. If it needs thickening, mix the cornflour in a small bowl with 50ml water. Stir this into the slow cooker mixture until it starts to thicken.

Spoon the crumble mixture over the top of the vegetable and bean mix. Put a tea towel over the top of the slow cooker, then pop on the lid and push down firmly to ensure that it forms a good seal. This will help to absorb any moisture and keep the crumble topping nice and crumbly.

Cook on low for a further 2–3 hours, or high for 1½ hours. Once cooked, you can brown the top, if you prefer, by putting the crock if it is ovenproof under a preheated grill for 5–8 minutes until golden. This does not enhance the flavour, but it's nice if you like a crunchy top. Serve with steamed green vegetables.

FOR THE CRUMBLE TOPPING

150g plain wholemeal flour

75g butter (or vegan butter), cut into small pieces

60g porridge oats

30g sunflower seeds

SPINACH & GOAT'S CHEESE STUFFED MUSHROOMS

SERVES 4

This dish could be a starter at a dinner party, but I have it as a main meal served with a lovely salad and drizzled with some balsamic vinegar. If you are not a fan of goat's cheese, you can swap it for feta or ricotta – both work well.

METHOD

Oil inside the slow cooker well to ensure the mushrooms don't stick. Remove the stalks from the mushrooms. Chop the stalks finely and put them in a large bowl.

Put the spinach in a colander and pour over boiling water from the kettle until wilted slightly. Squeeze out any excess water and put the spinach in the bowl with the mushroom stalks.

Add the goat's cheese. Season with pepper and a little nutmeg to taste, and combine well.

Put a tablespoon of tomato paste into the base of each mushroom, then spread it over the mushroom until covered. Add a few spoonfuls of the goat's cheese mixture to each.

Put the breadcrumbs and Parmesan in a small bowl and mix together. Season with salt and pepper to taste, and combine well. Cover the mushrooms with a sprinkle of the breadcrumb mixture.

Put in the base of the slow cooker. Put a tea towel over the top of the slow cooker, then pop on the lid and push down firmly to ensure that it forms a good seal.

Cook on high for 2–3 hours until the mushrooms and stuffing are cooked through. (If your cooker is old and food tends to catch in places or it has erratic heat, it is better to cook on low and for longer to avoid any burning edges.) Serve with a green salad and a drizzle of balsamic vinegar.

NUTRITIONAL INFORMATION PER SERVING

445 Kcals

35g fat

14g net carbohydrates

16g protein

INGREDIENTS

1–2 tbsp olive oil, for greasing

4 portobello mushrooms

80g baby leaf spinach

150g goat's cheese, crumbled

½ tsp freshly grated nutmeg, or to taste (optional)

4 tbsp sun-dried tomato paste

40g fresh breadcrumbs (or use stale bread)

30g vegetarian Parmesan cheese

salt and ground black pepper

green salad with a drizzle of balsamic vinegar, to serve

MOROCCAN VEGETABLE ONE POT

SERVES 4–6

NUTRITIONAL INFORMATION PER SERVING

(based on 6 servings)

290 Kcals

5.2g fat

39g net carbohydrates

14g protein

INGREDIENTS

1 red onion, chopped

2 garlic cloves, roughly chopped

1–2 chillies, to taste, deseeded (unless you like the extra heat), finely chopped

2cm piece of fresh ginger, peeled and finely chopped

2 red peppers, diced (*see* Tip)

1 large courgette, cut into chunks

1 celery stick, diced

1 carrot, diced

½ aubergine (optional), cut into chunks

2 × 400g tins chickpeas, drained and rinsed

400g tin chopped tomatoes

3 tsp ras el hanout

2 tsp chilli powder

½ tsp chilli flakes (optional)

1 tsp dried mint

400ml vegetable stock

a handful of ready-to-eat dried apricots, halved

couscous, to serve

The colours of this dish are so vibrant, plus it's healthy and delicious, with a little kick of heat, too. This is wonderful when served with couscous. If you wish to swap with other vegetable ingredients, you will find that most vegetables work well apart from swede, parsnip and potato, as they are too dense – so this is a great recipe to use up whatever you have in the fridge.

METHOD

Preheat your slow cooker following the manufacturer's instructions. Add all ingredients to the slow cooker apart from the apricots. Season with salt and pepper to taste, and combine well. Cook on low for 6–8 hours until the vegetables are tender. Thirty minutes before serving, add the apricots. Serve with couscous.

TIP

✳ *When preparing the vegetables, ensure that they are all evenly sized, as this helps with a more even cook, but keep the courgette and aubergine quite chunky.*

PUMPKIN RISOTTO

SERVES 4

Risottos work well in the slow cooker and this method of cooking takes the pressure off you, as you won't need to watch over it while it cooks. I have used pumpkin in this recipe, but it works well with any squash. This is a lovely, mild, creamy risotto, perfect for families.

METHOD

Preheat your slow cooker following the manufacturer's instructions. If your slow cooker has a sauté option, you can use this; if not, use a large saucepan. Put the olive oil and butter in the slow cooker or saucepan over a medium heat. Add the chopped onion and fry for 5 minutes or until translucent.

Put the onion mixture in the slow cooker. Add the pumpkin and stir well.

Add the rice and stir in 500ml hot stock.

Cook on high for 1–2 hours until the rice is tender but not soggy. Fifteen to thirty minutes before serving, season with salt and pepper and add the nutmeg, then stir in the grated Parmesan. Add more stock if the risotto still has too much bite. Cook until softened, adding more stock if needed. Serve with extra Parmesan.

NUTRITIONAL INFORMATION PER SERVING

267 Kcals

6.7g fat

43g net carbohydrates

7.2g protein

INGREDIENTS

1 tbsp olive oil

a knob of butter

1 onion, finely chopped

1 small pumpkin, peeled, deseeded and cubed (about 300g of flesh)

300g risotto/Arborio rice

500–700ml hot vegetable stock, as needed

¼ tsp freshly grated nutmeg

50g vegetarian Parmesan, grated, plus extra to serve

salt and ground black pepper

When we look at cutting our spending, one of the big things that families tend to overspend on is takeaways. According to Statista (which compiles consumer and market data), the UK spends a whopping £10.9 billion every year on takeaways, and the younger generations are the most likely to spend on these.

The quick-and-easy option of picking up the phone and having a meal delivered within the hour has its appeal, but when you look at the costs, as well as the health implications, it is a habit that we should all be trying to curb (most takeaways are not just calorie ridden but they are also full of salt, sugar and unhealthy fats).

This chapter proves that you can still have your takeaways, except that they are made at home in the slow cooker. You can also double up your recipe and create your own ready meals to pop into the freezer ready for when the urge for a takeaway grabs you.

SO-SIMPLE CHICKEN & CHICKPEA CURRY

SERVES 4

NUTRITIONAL INFORMATION PER SERVING

547 Kcals

29g fat

26g net carbohydrates

42g protein

INGREDIENTS

4–6 chicken legs (or thighs or 500g breast)

1 tbsp olive oil

3 garlic cloves, crushed

1 large onion, finely chopped

2 tbsp curry powder

400g tin chopped tomatoes

400g tin chickpeas, including liquid

250g coconut cream

salt and ground black pepper

rice and naan breads, to serve

This really is a very simple curry – a quick, throw-it-all-in recipe, but it tastes amazing. You can, if you have any to hand, add some defrosted frozen spinach or some chopped kale, but don't add this until the last hour of cooking.

METHOD

If you are using chicken legs or thighs, it is nicer to brown them before putting them in the slow cooker, especially if they have the skin on. You do not have to do this if you are using skinless thighs or breast. If your slow cooker has a sauté option, you can use this; if not, use a frying pan. Heat the oil in the slow cooker or in the frying pan over a medium-high heat. Fry the chicken for 5 minutes or until browned all over. Transfer to the slow cooker.

Add all the remaining ingredients, season with salt and pepper to taste, and combine well.

Cook on low for 6–8 hours. Serve with rice and naan breads.

CHICKEN BIRYANI

SERVES 4–6

NUTRITIONAL INFORMATION
PER SERVING

(based on 6 servings)

439 Kcals

15g fat

54g net carbohydrates

20g protein

INGREDIENTS

250ml carton coconut cream (not creamed coconut)

400g tin chopped tomatoes

4 garlic cloves

1 red chilli

2cm piece of fresh ginger, peeled and grated

½ tsp ground cinnamon

1 tsp ground cardamom

1–2 tbsp garam masala, to taste

1 tsp ground coriander

½ tsp ground cumin

1 tsp ground turmeric

2 tsp paprika

400g boneless, skinless chicken thighs, diced

1 onion, diced

1 red or yellow pepper, deseeded and diced

salt and ground black pepper

cucumber raita, to serve

A biryani has always been one of my favourite Indian meals. This is my quick-and-easy slow cooker adaptation of the classic, in a very simple form, but I think it still packs a punch!

METHOD

Preheat your slow cooker following the manufacturer's instructions. Put the coconut cream, tomatoes, garlic and all the spices into a food processor or blender and whizz until smooth.

Pour this in the slow cooker. Add the diced chicken, onion and diced pepper. Season with salt and pepper to taste, and combine well.

Cook on low for 6 hours. One hour before serving, cook your basmati rice. Put the rice in a large pan of boiling water over a medium-high heat, and add the turmeric, star anise, cloves and bay leaves. Cook for 10 minutes until almost tender. Drain well, and remove the star anise, cloves and bay leaves.

Put the rice on top of the chicken and stir to combine, or you can leave it just on the top if you prefer layers of flavour.

Turn up to high and cook for 30 minutes before serving. I serve this with some cooling cucumber raita (made with plain yoghurt, cucumber and chopped mint leaves).

FOR THE RICE

350g basmati rice, rinsed

½ tsp turmeric

1 star anise

4 cloves

2 bay leaves

CHICKEN TIKKA MASALA

SERVES 4

This is one of my favourite curries. I use boneless, skinless chicken thighs for added depth of flavour. You can cook most curries at least a day in advance, as they do generally improve with age (within reason) – ready to heat up when needed.

METHOD

Preheat your slow cooker following the manufacturer's instructions. Put the garlic into a food processor or blender and add the chillies, cardamom, cinnamon, coriander, tikka masala, tomatoes, tomato purée and coconut cream. Whizz until smooth.

Put the onion, red pepper and chicken in the slow cooker. Add the creamed liquid.

Cook on low for 6–7 hours or until the chicken is tender. Just before serving, stir in the fresh coriander leaves, leaving a few to garnish. Garnish and serve with basmati rice, cauliflower rice or flatbreads.

TIP

✳ *To make cauliflower rice, cut a cauliflower into florets and put into a food processor. Pulse until the cauliflower resembles rice. (Alternatively, use the large holes of a box grater, although this is messy and time-consuming.)*

To cook in a microwave, put the cauliflower rice into a container, without water, and cook on full power for 5–8 minutes (cooking times will depend on your microwave). Stir halfway through cooking to ensure an even cook. Remove and fluff up with a fork.

To cook on the hob, heat a little butter or coconut oil in saucepan. Add the cauliflower rice and toss gently over a medium heat for 5–8 minutes until heated through and softened.

NUTRITIONAL INFORMATION PER SERVING

503 Kcals

26g fat

21g net carbohydrates

38g protein

INGREDIENTS

2 garlic cloves

2 chillies, deseeded (unless you like the extra heat)

4 cardamom seeds

2 tsp ground cinnamon

1 tsp ground coriander

1 tbsp tikka masala curry powder (or medium curry powder)

2 tomatoes, quartered

3 tbsp tomato purée

250g carton of coconut cream (not creamed coconut)

1 onion, chopped

1 red pepper, deseeded and sliced

500g boneless, skinless chicken thighs, diced

a small handful of fresh coriander leaves

basmati rice, cauliflower rice or flatbreads, to serve

SWEET-&-SOUR PORK

SERVES 4

NUTRITIONAL INFORMATION
PER SERVING

374 Kcals

12g fat

31g net carbohydrates

30g protein

INGREDIENTS

500g pork, trimmed and cubed

1 onion, finely chopped

2 garlic cloves, crushed

1–2 red chillies, to taste, deseeded (unless you like the extra heat), finely sliced

3cm piece of fresh ginger, peeled and thinly sliced

1 red pepper, deseeded and roughly diced

1 green pepper, deseeded and roughly diced

2 heaped tsp cornflour

salt and ground black pepper

rice or noodles, to serve

FOR THE SAUCE

400g tin pineapple chunks in natural juice

2 tsp sesame oil

2 tbsp soy sauce

2 tbsp rice wine vinegar or white wine vinegar

2 tbsp tomato purée

1 tbsp brown sugar

250ml pork or chicken stock

salt and ground black pepper

This recipe uses diced pork, but if you prefer you can swap the pork for chicken. Simply follow the same format. If you like to have sweet-and-sour prawns, you can use this mixture, but it is better to cook them on the hob, as the prawns will only need a short cook.

METHOD

Preheat your slow cooker following the manufacturer's instructions. To make the sauce, first strain the pineapple chunks and reserve the juice.

Put the sesame oil in a jug and add the soy sauce, rice wine vinegar, tomato purée, brown sugar, pineapple juice and the stock. Combine well. Season with salt and pepper to taste.

Put the pork in the slow cooker and cover with the onion, garlic, chillies and ginger. Pour over the sauce. Season with salt and pepper to taste, and combine well.

Cook on low for 5–6 hours. One hour before serving, add the peppers and pineapple. Mix the cornflour in a small bowl with 50ml cold water. Stir this into the slow cooker mixture and combine well. Cook on high for 1 hour. Serve on a bed of rice or noodles.

SLOW-COOKED DONER KEBAB

SERVES 4

This is very easy to make and is much healthier than the takeaway alternative. Serve it with some salad in between pitta breads or flatbreads. This recipe uses minced lamb, but you can use minced beef, chicken or turkey for a variation.

METHOD

Preheat your slow cooker following the manufacturer's instructions. Put all the ingredients into a food processor and whizz until smooth.

Oil a square of foil, about 35cm, enough to wrap the meat tightly. Tip out the meat and form it into a thick sausage shape. Put onto the foil and wrap tightly.

Put the foiled meat into the slow cooker and cook on low for 5–6 hours. When ready to serve, unwrap the foil, remove the meat and put it on a chopping board. Thinly slice the kebab meat and serve it with salad stuffed into pitta or flatbreads.

NUTRITIONAL INFORMATION PER SERVING

413 Kcals

27g fat

2.9g net carbohydrates

39g protein

INGREDIENTS

750g minced lamb

½ onion, finely chopped

3 garlic cloves, crushed

2 tsp chilli powder, or to taste

1 tsp ground cumin

1 tsp ground coriander

2 tsp dried oregano

2 tsp smoked paprika

1 egg, beaten

salt and ground black pepper

pitta breads or flatbreads and salad, to serve

SIMPLE THAI GREEN CURRY

SERVES 4

NUTRITIONAL INFORMATION PER SERVING

492 Kcals

33g fat

7.1g net carbohydrates

41g protein

INGREDIENTS

1 onion, finely chopped

1–2 garlic cloves, to taste, roughly chopped

2cm piece of fresh ginger, peeled and finely chopped

juice and zest of ½ lime

2–3 tbsp Thai curry paste, to taste

400ml can coconut milk

600g skinless, boneless chicken, diced

80g baby leaf spinach

fresh coriander leaves, to garnish

jasmine rice, to serve

We all love simple recipes, and this is another where you can simply chuck it all in and leave it to cook – perfect for busy days. Although I normally make my own Thai curry paste, this recipe uses a shop-bought paste, as you might find it works out cheaper than making your own from scratch. You can get Thai green curry paste from your local supermarket, but check out the world food shops, as you can often buy it cheaper there. The recipe recommends that you use 2 tbsp, but much will depend on the heat of the paste, so use your judgement on this and add to taste.

METHOD

Preheat your slow cooker following the manufacturer's instructions. Put all the ingredients, except for the spinach, in the slow cooker.

Cook on low for 6–7 hours until the chicken is tender. Add the spinach leaves. Turn up to high and cook for 20 minutes. Garnish with coriander leaves and serve with jasmine rice.

CHICKEN VINDALOO

SERVES 4

This is quite a hot dish, so adjust the spices to suit your own taste. If you double up the recipe, you can freeze what you don't use, ready for another meal. You can use chicken breasts, chicken legs or thighs for this dish. Thighs are the most economical and the tastiest.

METHOD

Put all the ingredients, except the onion, chicken and stock, in a food processor or blender and whizz until you form a paste.

If you are marinating the meat, put the chicken in a bowl or freezer bag, pour on the paste and leave to marinate for at least 2 hours. Skip this step if you are not wanting to marinate.

Preheat your slow cooker following the manufacturer's instructions. Put the onion, chicken and paste in the slow cooker. Season with salt and combine well.

Cook on low for 6 hours. Serve with basmati rice or cauliflower rice and naan bread.

TIP

✳ *I like to marinate the chicken for at least 2 hours before putting it in the slow cooker. You don't have to do this, but I feel that it increases the flavour.*

NUTRITIONAL INFORMATION PER SERVING

260 Kcals

12.4g fat

5.7g net carbohydrates

30.9g protein

INGREDIENTS

2 tbsp olive oil

1 chilli

2 garlic cloves

2–4 tbsp vindaloo curry paste, to taste

1 tsp ground turmeric

1 tsp ground cumin

3 tomatoes

a small handful of fresh coriander leaves

1 large red onion, diced

600g chicken, diced (breast, leg or thigh)

250ml bone stock or chicken stock

salt

basmati rice or cauliflower rice (see page 185) and naan bread, to serve

CHICKEN CHOW MEIN

SERVES 4

NUTRITIONAL INFORMATION
PER SERVING

586 Kcals

14g fat

67g net carbohydrates

45g protein

INGREDIENTS

500g skinless, boneless chicken
thighs, cut into thin strips

1 onion, finely chopped

2 garlic cloves, crushed

1–2 red chillies, to taste, deseeded
(unless you like the extra heat),
finely sliced

3cm piece of fresh ginger, peeled
and thinly sliced

300g dried egg noodles

a drizzle of olive oil

chopped chilli, to garnish

FOR THE SAUCE

2 tbsp soy sauce

2 tbsp rice wine vinegar or
white wine vinegar

3 tbsp hoisin sauce

1 tsp Chinese five-spice powder

300ml chicken stock

salt and ground black pepper

You might not think about doing chicken chow mein in your slow cooker, but it is so easy and, most importantly, it's delicious!

METHOD

Preheat your slow cooker following the manufacturer's instructions. Put all the sauce ingredients in a jug. Season with salt and pepper to taste, and combine well.

Put the chicken in the slow cooker and cover with the onion, garlic, chillies and ginger. Pour over the sauce.

Cook on low for 5–6 hours until the chicken is tender. Thirty minutes before serving, cook the egg noodles in a saucepan of boiling water for 8–10 minutes, or according to the pack instructions. Drain and toss them in a little oil to prevent them from sticking together. Add the noodles to the slow cooker and combine well before serving, garnished with chilli.

TIP

✳ *It's hardly authentic, but you can swap noodles for regular pasta if you prefer.*

JALFREZI CHICKEN

SERVES 4

This is a really easy jalfrezi: I just chuck all the sauce ingredients into my food processor and then let them do their magic in the slow cooker. If you like the 'chuck it in and go away' style of cooking, this one is for you. You can also double up the sauce mixture and freeze it, or double up the whole recipe and freeze it to create your own ready meals.

METHOD

Preheat your slow cooker following the manufacturer's instructions. Put the sauce ingredients into a food processor or blender and whizz until combined.

Put the chicken, onion and red peppers in the slow cooker and pour over the sauce.

Cook on low for 6–7 hours until the chicken is tender. Thirty minutes before serving, mix the cornflour in a small bowl with 50ml cold water. Stir this into the slow cooker mixture and combine well. Cook on high for 30 minutes. Serve with basmati rice and flatbreads.

NUTRITIONAL INFORMATION PER SERVING

159 Kcals

29g fat

17g net carbohydrates

45g protein

INGREDIENTS

600g skinless, boneless chicken, diced

1 onion, chopped

2 red peppers, deseeded and thickly diced

1 tbsp cornflour

basmati rice and flatbreads, to serve

FOR THE SAUCE

400g tin chopped tomatoes

3 garlic cloves

3cm piece of fresh ginger, peeled and grated

2 chillies, deseeded (unless you like the extra heat), finely sliced

3 tsp ground cumin

4 tsp ground coriander

1 tsp ground turmeric

2 tsp garam masala

1 tbsp tomato purée

250g coconut cream

150ml chicken stock

salt and ground black pepper

FRAGRANT BEEF RENDANG CURRY

SERVES 6

NUTRITIONAL INFORMATION PER SERVING

381 Kcals

22g fat

12g net carbohydrates

31g protein

INGREDIENTS

2 tsp coconut oil

750g stewing steak, thickly diced

1 large red onion, thickly chopped

2 red peppers, deseeded and cut into large chunks

salt

basmati or Thai rice, to serve

FOR THE CURRY PASTE

4cm piece of fresh ginger, peeled and grated

4 garlic cloves

3 chillies, deseeded (unless you like the extra heat), finely sliced

2 lemongrass stalks, hard outer leaves and top third removed, chopped

4cm piece of fresh galangal, peeled

4 cardamom pods

4 kaffir lime leaves

1 tsp fennel seeds

2 tsp coriander seeds

1 tsp cumin seeds

1 lime, zest and juice

2 tsp ground cinnamon

½ tsp ground ginger

1 tsp hot paprika

1 tsp ground turmeric

1 tbsp honey

400g tin coconut milk

Don't let the long ingredients list put you off this traditional Malaysian beef curry. It's a brilliant recipe, which is impressive and flavoursome but it's also easy to make. Most supermarkets sell fresh lemongrass and galangal, but if you can't buy fresh, you can buy these flavourings in jars. As long as you have a food processor or blender the curry paste is simplicity itself. Just like other spicy recipes, this curry does improve with age, so it is often best on the second day.

METHOD

Preheat the slow cooker following the manufacturer's instructions. Put the curry paste ingredients into a food processor or blender and whizz until they are all combined and form a smooth paste.

If your slow cooker has a sauté option, you can use this; if not, use a frying pan. Heat the oil in the slow cooker or in the frying pan over a medium-high heat. Add the steak and cook for 5 minutes or until it is brown all over, sealing in the meat and flavour. Put in the slow cooker and add the curry paste, onion and peppers. Season with salt to taste and combine well.

Cook on low for 8 hours. Serve with basmati or Thai rice.

TIP

✳ *You can also double up the curry paste and store it in the freezer ready to pop out whenever you fancy a curry.*

Desserts

We don't always think about making desserts in the slow cooker, but they can be really delicious and so easy: you can make successful puddings, desserts and even cakes. I love my slow cooker so much that I actually have a small slow cooker that I use only for desserts.

If you are new to slow cooking, I strongly advise that you read the following advice on how the slow cooker works for desserts, cakes and sponge puddings. This is really important to ensure success.

CAKES AND SPONGES

When cooked in a slow cooker cakes and sponges will not have the same light texture as they do when baked, but they are still delicious and are ideal to serve as a dessert. The slow cooker can sometimes get quite wet inside, especially with the condensation that cooking creates. To prevent this from affecting your cakes or sponges see page 204.

DIETARY SWAPS

Many of us are becoming more health conscious. Some gluten-free, vegan and sugar-free ingredients can often mean that the recipe does not work as well as it might, but here are my top tips to convert any recipe into your way of eating.

Gluten-free We have some fantastic flours available now, and my favourite is from Doves Farm. You can swap like for like when you use this and gain great results, although I have found that adding about 30ml more liquid when using gluten-free flour for cakes and sponge puddings will give a much better result. Some of the dessert recipes in this book contain suet; check the labels, but you can buy gluten-free as well as vegetarian suet (suet is coated with flour to stop it from sticking together).

Vegan You can buy vegan margarines that work as a direct swap for butter. You can also use coconut oil. For a milk swap, switch to almond, coconut or rice milk.

With respect to eggs, you can buy an egg replacement, but I use my own version: mix 1 tbsp flax or chia seeds with 1 tbsp water in a small bowl, leave it to soak and use this as a binder. You can also use nut butters, stewed fruit or mashed banana as egg replacers. Cashew nuts are very good for vegan cooking, as they can be soaked to form a very creamy base, which is ideal for desserts or even soups. One of the dessert recipes uses suet, but you can opt for vegetarian suet.

Sugar-free Some readers might already know that this is my passion, and I have written several books on sugar-free diets. I have worked with dozens of schools, reducing their sugar intake by as much as 40 per cent in cakes and desserts without anyone noticing any change in their enjoyment of the dish. You really don't need things to be as sugary as they often are, so please bear this in mind when you are using these recipes.

You can reduce the sweetness to suit your palate as you become accustomed to eating fewer sweet foods. Start gradually and reduce, allowing you and your family to adjust to this change in your diet, which will in time reduce your sweet cravings. You can also opt for natural sweeteners that don't spike your blood sugar and are low in fructose, such as erythritol, xylitol, monk fruit granules and stevia. Erythritol also comes as an icing sugar replacement, as brown sugar and also in syrup form (known as fibre syrup). You can also use stevia in granule or liquid form, but this is over 300 times sweeter than sugar so it can be hard to gauge to taste.

If you are reducing your sugar, remember that natural sugars, such as bananas, dates, dried fruit, fruit juices, honey, maple syrup, agave syrup, coconut sugar, and so on, are all still packed with glucose and fructose, so it is only a sideways step if you use them. You will need to cut these down or avoid them altogether in order to keep your blood sugar low. For more information and great recipes, check out my website www.everydaysugarfree.co.uk

Fat These recipes call for butter or margarine. I am a fan of butter as I prefer natural foods, and butter is not as inflammatory as man-made fats, but you can opt for whatever suits your budget and health objective. I am also a huge fan of the low-carb way of eating, where we keep our fats high and our carbohydrates and sugars very low. You can look at reducing the sugar/carbs by making some swaps to natural sweeteners and switching flour to a nut-based flour such as ground almonds or coconut flour.

HOW TO GET A PUDDING BASIN IN AND OUT OF THE SLOW COOKER

Puddings are great in a slow cooker but it can be tricky getting them in and out without burning yourself. To avoid accidents, you can make yourself an easy string handle or a foil strap:

String handle If I'm using string to tie the top of a basin, I cut a second piece, about 40cm long, and double it. I then loop it around the string tied to either side of the top of the basin and tie it in the middle to form a handle.

Foil strap Simply cut a sheet of foil large enough to fit around the pudding basin and to give you enough to hold on to. I usually opt for 40–50cm. Fold the foil lengthways until you have a strong strap about 5cm wide. Put the bowl in the centre of the strap and fold the excess over the top. Put the bowl in your slow cooker and, when you need to remove it, simply unfold the straps and lift it out.

HOW TO STOP CAKES AND SPONGES GETTING SOGGY IN A SLOW COOKER

Put a tea towel over the top of the slow cooker, then pop on the lid and push down firmly to ensure that it forms a good seal. This stops the cake from getting too wet due to the steam created in the cooker. This technique is also good for when you want to create a dry, crisp edge to your food. This is not necessary if you are slow cooking a pudding with a foil or parchment lid, however.

APPLE & PEAR CRUMBLE

SERVES 6

Early autumn is when apples are in abundance and people with apple trees often leave unwanted apples for neighbours to help themselves to. These can be peeled and frozen, in order to last you the rest of the year. I like to mix eating apples with cooking apples, but just use up what you have. This recipe is also great to use up any apples and pears that have been left in the fruit bowl and become brown or bruised. If you don't have pears to hand, you can use tinned.

This is an all-in-one slow cooker crumble, but if you prefer a crispy crumble top, you can cook the fruit in the slow cooker without the crumble topping and add this before popping the crock, if it is ovenproof, into your conventional oven for 15 minutes for the top to crisp up.

METHOD

Preheat the slow cooker following the manufacturer's instructions. Put the apples and pears in the slow cooker, add the sugar, 3 tbsp water and the butter, and combine well.

Cook on high for 30 minutes to help to soften the fruit.

Meanwhile, prepare the crumble topping. Mix the flour and sugar together in a bowl, then rub in the butter using your fingertips until it resembles breadcrumbs.

Spoon the crumble evenly over the apple mixture. Put a tea towel over the top of the slow cooker, then pop on the lid and push down firmly to ensure that it forms a good seal to stop condensation, which can make the topping soggy.

Cook on low for 2 hours. Serve with homemade custard.

TIP

✴ *You can double up this recipe and use the remaining stewed fruit to make another crumble to pop into the freezer.*

NUTRITIONAL INFORMATION PER SERVING

503 Kcals

12g fat

90g net carbohydrates

5.8g protein

INGREDIENTS

4 apples (can be eating or cooking apples, or a combination), peeled, cored and thickly diced

2 pears, peeled, cored and thickly diced

50g sugar

25g butter or margarine

homemade custard, to serve

FOR THE CRUMBLE TOPPING

300g plain flour

150g sugar

150g cold butter or margarine, cut into pieces

ORANGE, CRANBERRY & APPLE CAKE

SERVES 8

NUTRITIONAL INFORMATION PER SERVING

374 Kcals

19g fat

47g net carbohydrates

2.7g protein

INGREDIENTS

180g butter or margarine, cut into pieces, plus extra for greasing

160g sugar

3 eggs

190g self-raising flour

1–2 tsp ground cinnamon, to taste

1 cooking apple, peeled, cored and diced

zest of 2 oranges

125g dried cranberries

icing sugar, for sprinkling

This cake is great at any time of the year, but it is particularly good at Christmas as a lighter option to a Christmas cake. This cake is very forgiving – it works well however you change it. I use dried cranberries, but you can use raisins or sultanas if you prefer. For this recipe I am using a loaf tin, but if you don't have one, you can use three loaf-shaped cake liners (which help to hold the shape).

METHOD

Preheat your slow cooker following the manufacturer's instructions. Grease a 450g loaf tin or use three loaf-shaped cake liners. Put the butter in a food mixer and add the sugar, eggs and self-raising flour. Mix well until it forms a batter. (Alternatively, use a large bowl and cream the butter and sugar until pale using an electric beater or a wooden spoon, gradually beat in the eggs and then stir in the flour until well combined.)

Add the cinnamon, apple, orange zest and cranberries. Use a spoon to combine well.

Put the cake mixture into your prepared loaf tin and put the tin in the slow cooker.

Put a tea towel over the top of the slow cooker, then pop on the lid and push down firmly to ensure that it forms a good seal to stop condensation.

Cook on low for 4–5 hours, or on high for 2½–3 hours until firm in the centre and the top of the cake is dry. (Timings will vary depending on your machine.)

Carefully remove the cake from the slow cooker. Turn out onto a cooling rack and leave to cool completely. Sprinkle with icing sugar and serve.

MUM'S SIMPLE BREAD & BUTTER PUDDING

SERVES 6

My mum used to make this for us when we were children, as it is a very cheap-and-cheerful pudding, great for using up leftover bread, milk and eggs. It is still one of my favourite comfort foods. It cooks well in the slow cooker but does benefit from being browned in the oven for 15 minutes before serving if, like me, you love the crisp edges to contrast with the soft, sweet centre of the pudding. If your slow cooker crock is ovenproof, you can simply cook it in that and lift it out to brown in the oven or under the grill. If your crock is not ovenproof and you want a crispy top to the pudding, use an ovenproof dish that will fit inside the slow cooker.

METHOD

Preheat your slow cooker following the manufacturer's instructions. Butter the base of your slow cooker or ovenproof dish.

Put the milk in a bowl and add the eggs, orange zest and mixed spice. Mix together well.

Put a layer of buttered bread in your slow cooker or dish, then sprinkle with sultanas and a fine sprinkling of sugar. Make two more layers. Pour over the milk mixture.

Put a tea towel over the top of the slow cooker, then pop on the lid and push down firmly to ensure that it forms a good seal to stop condensation.

Cook on low for 3–4 hours until cooked through and soft. Serve immediately, or if you prefer a very crispy top, transfer the crock or ovenproof dish to the oven preheated to 180°C (160°C fan oven) Gas 4, or pop under a preheated grill to brown the top until crispy and golden. Serve with a dollop of cream, crème fraîche or Greek yoghurt.

NUTRITIONAL INFORMATION PER SERVING

343 Kcals

9g fat

51g net carbohydrates

13g protein

INGREDIENTS

butter for greasing

500ml whole milk

3 large eggs

zest of 1 orange

1 tsp ground mixed spice

10 slices of white bread (can be slightly stale), buttered, cut into quarters

100g sultanas

50g sugar

whipped cream, crème fraîche or Greek yoghurt, to serve

TIP

✳ *You can use any bread, including stale bread, fruit breads, hot cross buns, or even leftover Christmas panettone. You can also vary the flavours, using chocolate chips, raspberries, banana or chunks of apple.*

CHOCOLATE CHIP BANANA BREAD

SERVES 10

NUTRITIONAL INFORMATION
PER SERVING

346 Kcals

8.3g fat

59g net carbohydrates

7.8g protein

INGREDIENTS

butter, for greasing

5 ripe bananas

400g tin sweetened
condensed milk

320g self-raising flour

1 tsp ground cinnamon

40g walnuts, finely chopped

60g dark chocolate chips

This is the perfect recipe for using up overripe bananas. You can even use frozen bananas for this, just make sure that you defrost them first. I have added some chocolate chips, as this is a big favourite with children, but for a more grown-up version, you could add more chopped walnuts or pecan nuts along with a little more cinnamon.

METHOD

Preheat your slow cooker following the manufacturer's instructions. Grease a 450g loaf tin or use three loaf-shaped cake liners. (You can also put the cake directly into your slow cooker, as long as you thoroughly grease and line the crock; this will produce a flatter cake, depending on the size of your slow cooker, but it will still taste delicious.) Mash the ripe bananas and put them in a bowl. Add the milk and flour, and mix well.

Add the cinnamon, walnuts and chocolate chips, and give the mixture a final stir.

Put the mixture into the prepared tin or cake liners (or on the base of the crock), spreading the mixture evenly, and put it in the slow cooker.

Put a tea towel over the top of the slow cooker, then pop on the lid and push down firmly to ensure that it forms a good seal to stop condensation.

Cook on low for 3–4 hours, or on high for 2–2½ hours, or until firm in the centre. (Timings will vary depending on your machine. Older machines may cook unevenly and can catch in places, in which case I would recommend cooking on low and using liners.)

CHOCOLATE SELF-SAUCING PUDDING

SERVES 6

This is one of those puddings that you can make out of store-cupboard ingredients but feels indulgent and comforting, and it has its own lovely soft sauce when you turn it out.

METHOD

Preheat your slow cooker following the manufacturer's instructions. Grease a 1.2 litre pudding basin thoroughly with butter. Put the butter and sugar in a mixing bowl and cream together until pale using an electric beater or wooden spoon. Add 1 egg and beat well, then sift in some of the flour and cocoa, and beat well again. Continue in this way with the other eggs, flour and cocoa until it is all incorporated.

Put the cake mixture into the pudding basin.

To make the sauce, mix the cocoa, sugar and 175ml water together in a bowl, and pour this over the sponge mixture.

Cover the pudding basin with baking parchment and a layer of foil, and tie very securely with string. (I like to use a double-sided parchment from Lakeland with foil on one side and parchment on the other.) It is advisable to make a handle with string to make it easier to lift the pudding in and out of the slow cooker (see page 204).

Boil the kettle. Put the pudding in the base of your slow cooker, then add enough boiling water until it comes halfway up the side of the basin.

Cook on high for 2½–3 hours, or 5–6 hours on low, until the sponge springs back when gently pressed. Remove from the slow cooker. Run a knife around the edge of the bowl. Put a plate on the top of the bowl and carefully flip it over, to turn out the pudding. Serve with homemade custard, ice cream or crème fraîche.

NUTRITIONAL INFORMATION PER SERVING

495 Kcals

22g fat

62g net carbohydrates

11g protein

INGREDIENTS

200g butter or margarine, plus extra for greasing

150g sugar

4 eggs

180g self-raising flour

40g cocoa powder

homemade custard, ice cream or crème fraîche, to serve

FOR THE SAUCE

50g cocoa powder

75g sugar

ORANGE & CINNAMON PUDDING

SERVES 6

NUTRITIONAL INFORMATION
PER SERVING

442 Kcals

16g fat

64g net carbohydrates

7.9g protein

INGREDIENTS

175g butter or margarine,
plus extra for greasing

150g sugar

3 large eggs

220g self-raising flour

100g mixed dried fruit

zest of 1 orange

2 tsp ground cinnamon

1 tsp ground mixed spice

homemade custard, ice cream
or crème fraîche, to serve

This pudding brings back childhood memories for me. It is comfort food at its best and perfect when served with homemade custard. It reminds me of a very light Christmas pudding with those wintery flavours but without the density.

METHOD

Preheat your slow cooker following the manufacturer's instructions. Grease a 1.2 litre pudding basin thoroughly with butter and leave to one side. You can also put a circle of parchment about the size of an orange at the base of the bowl if you are worried about it sticking. Cream the butter and sugar in a mixing bowl until pale using an electric beater or a wooden spoon. Add 1 egg and beat well, then sift in some of the flour, and beat well again. Continue in this way with the other eggs and flour until it is all incorporated.

Add the dried fruit, orange zest, cinnamon and mixed spice, and stir well.

Put the mixture into the prepared pudding basin. Cover the top with baking parchment and a layer of foil, and tie very securely with string. It is advisable to make a handle with string to make it easy to lift the pudding in and out of the slow cooker (see page 204).

Boil the kettle. Put the pudding in the base of your slow cooker, then add enough boiling water until it comes halfway up the side of the basin.

Cook on high for 2–3 hours, or 4–6 hours on low, until the sponge springs back when lightly pressed. Remove from the slow cooker. Run a knife around the edge of the basin. Place a plate on the top of the bowl and carefully flip it over, to turn out the pudding. Serve with homemade custard, ice cream or crème fraîche.

RICE PUDDING WITH RASPBERRY SAUCE

SERVES 6

I get cravings for a milky pudding whenever I'm feeling under par. Rice pudding is incredibly comforting and can be very cheap to make. When I was at school, we used to have a lovely creamy rice pudding with a dollop of raspberry jam. This recipe is a nod to that time, but with a very simple homemade raspberry sauce.

If you are vegan, you could swap the milk for coconut milk and add a carton of vegan cream to create a creamy consistency and flavour.

METHOD

Preheat your slow cooker following the manufacturer's instructions. Grease the slow cooker with butter or use a slow cooker liner. Put the milk, rice, sugar and vanilla, if using, in the slow cooker. Dot with the 1 tbsp butter.

Cook on low for 5–6 hours; stir the mixture every now and again to prevent the rice from sticking or cooking in lumps.

Meanwhile to make the raspberry sauce, put the raspberries in a saucepan over a medium heat. Add 50ml water and heat gently until the raspberries start to break down. Add sugar to taste. You can keep the sauce like this or you can sieve it to remove the seeds. Put in a bowl until ready to serve.

When the rice is cooked, add the cream and cook on high for 15 minutes, stirring occasionally. Add more milk if needed until you get the consistency you desire.

Serve the rice pudding sprinkled with nutmeg and drizzled with some of the raspberry sauce. You can decorate with fresh raspberries if you wish.

NUTRITIONAL INFORMATION PER SERVING

377 Kcals

26g fat

28g net carbohydrates

7g protein

INGREDIENTS

1 tbsp butter, plus extra for greasing

1 litre whole milk, plus extra if needed

80g pudding rice

3 tbsp caster sugar

1 tsp vanilla paste (optional)

200ml double cream

a sprinkle of freshly grated nutmeg (optional)

fresh raspberries (optional), to decorate

FOR THE RASPBERRY SAUCE

100g frozen raspberries

1 tbsp sugar, or to taste

CARROT CAKE WITH MASCARPONE ICING

SERVES 10

NUTRITIONAL INFORMATION PER SERVING

511 Kcals

28g fat

57g net carbohydrates

5.2g protein

INGREDIENTS

butter, for greasing

200g self-raising flour

½ tsp bicarbonate of soda

1 tsp ground cinnamon

1½ tsp ground coriander

½ tsp freshly grated nutmeg

150g brown sugar

130ml light olive oil

3 eggs, beaten

200g carrots, grated

75g sultanas

40g desiccated coconut

FOR THE MASCARPONE ICING

200g icing sugar

80g butter

100g mascarpone cheese

1 tsp vanilla paste

Cakes made in the slow cooker have a slightly dense sponge, so this way of cooking works well with carrot cake and fruit cakes. This cake is topped with mascarpone butter icing, but you can use any vanilla butter icing.

METHOD

Preheat your slow cooker following the manufacturer's instructions. Grease and line the slow cooker or use a slow cooker liner. (I prefer to use three cake liners in the base of my slow cooker.) Or, if your slow cooker is large enough, you can use a cake tin, greased and lined with baking parchment. Sift the flour, bicarbonate of soda and spices into a large mixing bowl and stir in the sugar. In a separate bowl or jug, mix the oil, 60ml water and the eggs together.

Pour the wet mixture into the dry ingredients and combine until it forms a batter. Add the grated carrots, sultanas and coconut.

Put the cake mixture directly in your slow cooker or into the liner(s) or prepared cake tin. Put a tea towel over the top of the slow cooker, then pop on the lid and push down firmly to ensure that it forms a good seal.

Cook for 4–5 hours on low or on high for 2½–3 hours until firm in the centre and the top of the cake is dry. (Timings will vary depending on your machine. Older machines may cook more unevenly and can catch in places, in which case I would recommend cooking on low and using liners.)

Carefully remove the cake from the slow cooker and turn out onto a cooling rack to cool completely before adding your icing.

To make the icing, cream the icing sugar and butter together in a food mixer, or in a bowl using an electric beater or wooden spoon. When it is starting to get nice and creamy, add the mascarpone with the vanilla paste, and combine again until it is light and creamy. Do not over-beat.

Smooth over the top of the cooled carrot cake and serve.

STORE-CUPBOARD BAKED APPLES

SERVES 4

This recipe uses dessert apples, such as Gala, but you can use cooking apples if you prefer a sharper flavour. I have used some store-cupboard finds to stuff these apples, but almost anything works: dried fruit, oats, nuts, granola, muesli, mincemeat or even some other fruits such as frozen berries.

METHOD

Preheat your slow cooker following the manufacturer's instructions. Partially core the apples; try not to go all the way through the apple, leaving some core on the base to prevent the stuffing from pouring out of the apples once they're in the slow cooker. Leave the skin intact. Cut a 'lid' from the top of the apples and set aside.

Put the oats in a bowl and add the pecan nuts, dried fruit and spices. Put 1 tsp jam in the base of each of the apples. Follow with the oat mixture. Place 1 tsp butter on top of the oats.

Drizzle with the honey and pop on the apple lid. Put in your slow cooker. Pour 200ml water around the apples.

Cook on low for 3–4 hours until the apples are soft. Serve with crème fraîche or natural yoghurt.

NUTRITIONAL INFORMATION PER SERVING

304 Kcals

13g fat

42g net carbohydrates

2.2g protein

INGREDIENTS

4 whole apples (preferably dessert variety, such as Gala, but cooking apples work well too), unpeeled

4 tbsp oats (or muesli)

2 tbsp pecan nuts, chopped

3 tbsp dried fruit

1 tsp ground cinnamon

½ tsp ground mixed spice

4 tsp raspberry or blackberry jam

4 tsp butter

2–4 tbsp clear honey

full-fat crème fraîche or natural yoghurt

RECIPE INDEX

INDEX

V

W